SUSTAINING CORPORATE GROWTH

Harnessing Your Strategic Strengths

D1508643

SUSTAINING CORPORATE GROWTH
Harnessing Your Strategic Strengths

by

A.T. KEARNEY, INC.

S^t_L

St. Lucie Press

Boca Raton London New York Washington, D.C.

Library of Congress Cataloging-in-Publication Data

Sustaining corporate growth : harnessing your strategic strengths / by A.T. Kearney, Inc.
    p. cm.
    Includes bibliographical references and index.
    ISBN 1-57444-289-9 (alk. paper)
    1. Corporations—Growth—Case studies. 2. Technological innovations—Economic aspects—Case studies. 3. Industrial management—Case studies. I. A.T. Kearney, Inc.

HD2746 .S87 2000
658.4'06—dc21
                                                  00-036609
                                                      CIP

© 2000 by A.T. Kearney, Inc.
St. Lucie Press is an imprint of CRC Press LLC

No claim to original U.S. Government works
International Standard Book Number 1-57444-289-9
Library of Congress Card Number 00-036609
Printed in the United States of America 1 2 3 4 5 6 7 8 9 0
Printed on acid-free paper

FOREWORD

Shareholder value ... hypergrowth ...
virtuous cycle ... globalization ...

From the boardroom to the mail room, the lexicon of growth has become the *lingua franca* of today's business world as executives everywhere look for a prescription for success in the increasingly competitive global economy. But in this rush for a secret recipe for expansion and growth, many may have overlooked an unlikely, but perhaps necessary, ingredient: adversity.

The corporate success stories found in this book paint a simple but powerful picture. In almost every case, the businesses profiled found that the key to their phenomenal growth lay in overcoming a profound competitive disadvantage. The relative isolation and small population base of Singapore Airlines' home airport drove the carrier to rely on unsurpassed customer service to attract passengers. Carlton and United Breweries used Australia's changing demographics as a spur to innovate and diversify, and, in the process, became the largest brewer "down under." Facing expiring drug patents and a sparse pipeline, Bristol-Myers Squibb defied Wall Street's conventional wisdom by pushing productivity to free up internal funds and emphasizing continued research and development.

Each of these companies found that they developed their potential for growth by battling odds that threatened their very survival. In the process, they came to regard their initial disadvantages as the secret source of their ensuing strength. This echoes Sam Walton's evaluation of the early stages of creating the world's largest retailer, Wal-Mart:

Here we were in the boondocks. We didn't have distributors falling over themselves to serve us like our competitors did in larger towns. Our only alternative was to build our own warehouses so we could buy in volume at attractive prices and store the merchandise.   — Sam Walton, *Forbes* Magazine, October 10, 1987

Competitive forces never stop. Just when a company finds itself near the top of the *Fortune 500*, new competitors and new competitive issues arise. Today, the competition often comes from e-business.

No one can develop a constant formula for growth — whether the challenge is e-commerce or another business revolution as-yet unforeseen. But if there is no permanent roadmap for growth, there are at least signposts along the way, and some of them can be found in the stories of courage, strength, and innovation in the case studies of this book.

Fred Steingraber
Chairman and CEO
A.T. Kearney, Inc.
November 1999

CONTRIBUTORS

Eike Bär
Motorola
Germany

Khoo Teng Chye
PSA Corporation Limited
Singapore

Christopher Clarke
A.T. Kearney, Inc.
Singapore

Nuno D'Aquino
Carlton and United Breweries
Australia

Jürgen Haritz
Bertelsmann Book Corporation
Germany

Brian Harrison
A. T. Kearney, Inc.
Canada

Archie Livis
Braun
Germany

Dieter Rams
Braun
Germany

Thomas Shin
A.T. Kearney, Inc.
South Korea

Doug Tunnell
Bristol-Myers Squibb
United States

Andrej Vizjak
Bertelsmann Book Corporation
Germany

ACKNOWLEDGMENTS

It takes many people, all over the world, to create a book with the scope of this one. By definition, a book that encapsulates the histories and business techniques of world-class companies headquartered around the world can only be pulled together by a team of people with deep business insights who are similarly located in business communities around the world. A.T. Kearney, the management consulting subsidiary of EDS, a leader in the global information technology services industry for more than 35 years, has that expertise and reach.

The genesis of this book was in Düsseldorf, Germany. There, Karl Deutsch and Eva Diedrichs coauthored the book, *Gewinnen mit Kernkompetenzen* (Carl Hanser Verlag) in 1997. The members of A.T. Kearney's Global Strategy Initiative encouraged them to produce an international version. Eva tapped the global A.T. Kearney network and compiled case studies from around the world.

In Asia-Pacific, A.T. Kearney consultants who helped develop the cases in this volume include Jim McGrath, Peter Munro, and Richard Comber (Australia); Christopher J. Clarke and Mui-Fong Goh (Singapore); and Thomas Shin (South Korea). Similarly, Robert Hutchens, Maximilian Schroeck, and David Rader were instrumental in developing the ideas behind the cases in North America.

Countless executives of the companies profiled on these pages graciously opened their doors and gave us time and energy to make this project possible. In addition to the authors who specifically wrote the articles, the heartwarming support of Dr. Cheong Choong Kong, chief executive director of Singapore Airlines, deserves special mention.

Turning the different chapters into a cohesive manuscript and getting that manuscript to the publisher proved to be equally challenging. Those challenges were ably met in Düsseldorf by Eva

Diedrichs with the support of Sven Gerlach, and in Chicago by a team comprising Lee Anne Petry, Patricia Sibo, Douglas Mose, and Paul Solans, under the direction of Martha H. Peak.

However, the work of all these people would have been fruitless without the leadership and sponsorship of Brian Harrison, A.T. Kearney's vice president of Global Support, based in Toronto. From the beginning, he envisioned a book that would incorporate A.T. Kearney's best thinking about long-term growth and the business strategies of the companies that, over the long haul and through good times and bad, earn the label of world class. Without his enthusiasm and direction — and yes, occasional nagging — this book could never have become a reality.

Chicago
November 1999

CONTENTS

Introduction

WRITING THE STORIES
OF SUCCESS

Brian Harrison

The classic Brothers Grimm nursery story of "Jack and the Beanstalk" reads like a business dream come true: a risky deal promises great returns, is scorned by skeptics, and ultimately results in phenomenal growth and profits. Of course, Jack meets a few obstacles along the way, but he overcomes these through flexibility and innovative thinking.

In the business world, Jack's fairy-tale experience is mirrored in the experiences of a select group of companies. Larger-than-life growth — accompanied by risk, obstacles, and incredible profits—is the common element of the companies examined in this book. And with growth becoming increasingly essential to creating and maintaining shareholder value, such stellar examples have much to teach the rest of us.

Growth — and the promise of growth — is paramount for investors. Traditional performance indicators such as earnings and cash flow, while important, are no longer the primary determining factors in stock valuations. Instead, companies that actively pursue and generate revenue growth are far more likely to achieve a high and sustainable share price.

This book profiles eight companies that have remarkable growth stories and outstanding track records of shareholder value creation: Singapore Airlines, Bristol-Myers Squibb, Braun, Motorola, Carlton and United Breweries, SK Telecom, Bertelsmann, and the Port of Singapore Authority. This is a diverse group of companies from a broad range of industries that have vastly different cultural and geographic backgrounds. Their stories illustrate the spectrum of approaches to growth — from acquisitions and alliances to product innovation, customer service, and brand management — that set them apart from their competitors. In many of these cases you will find real examples of traditional growth strategies, such as creating first mover advantage, leveraging core competencies, and harnessing increasing returns to scale.

As we compiled and edited these stories, five themes emerged — common threads that run through very distinct chronicles of success:

1. *Challenge.* There are no "slam dunks" in this book, no easy wins. Each of the companies profiled faced and overcame significant adversity to reach its world-class status. Pressures on these businesses variously included the devastation of war, the competitive pressures of deregulation, regional economic crises, stock market crashes, inability to raise capital, expiry of critical patents, attacks by powerful competitors, and declining demand for core products. But all rose above these challenges to consistently outperform the market.

2. *Vision.* Many of these companies attribute their growth to a compelling business idea — a driving preconception of the market and competitive uniqueness that propelled their success. Each vision provided focus, unity, and energy to the company's drive to overcome adversity and achieve growth objectives. These visions are not bland statements of corporate purpose that collect dust in office lobbies. They are clear, believable statements of how we are going to win. Singapore Airlines' remarkable growth story began with "a vision to develop SIA into a unique airline offering the highest quality of service in the business." Nuno D'Aquino describes how Carlton and United Breweries' turnaround began with a "lead enterprise" vision. These visions, and the others described here, had the power to focus and energize the people who needed to "make it happen."

3. *The customer.* Mundane as the term is, each of these companies grounded their exceptional growth in customer focus. Each prides itself on its deep and penetrating understanding of what

its customers need, want, or expect, and on an unflinching commitment to deliver against that expectation. Author Eike Bär links the growth of Motorola's Land Mobile Products Sector to the division's success at maintaining close relationships with end users and focusing its R&D programs on emerging customer needs. The Port of Singapore Authority places "attention to customer needs" as the foremost element of its strategic vision. These companies grow because their customers want to buy their products and services.

4. *Excellence*. The terms "world class," "benchmarking," and "best practice" echo through the cases in this book. All of the companies profiled here exemplify excellence in the products and services they offer and beyond. Each has a particular ability (or abilities) at which it excels. But vision, customer focus, and the ability to overcome challenges mean little if, at its core, a company is simply mediocre. Jürgen Haritz and Andrej Vizjak link Bertelsmann's competitiveness in the book club industry today to the "World Class Performance Program" the company founded and developed. Archie Livis and Dieter Rams trace Braun's remarkable growth to its commitment to product superiority.

5. *Learning*. For all these companies, the ability to grow emerged from the ability to learn new markets, new strategies, and new technologies. Doug Tunnell shares several examples of how Bristol-Myers Squibb is obtaining unexpected synergies by pushing new skills and knowledge across the organization. Thomas Shin's story of SK Telecom is one of remarkable learning and adaptation to stay on top in the rapidly changing world of mobile telephony. As Nuno D'Aquino succinctly put it in his discussion of Carlton Breweries: "An organization's only sustainable competitive advantage is its ability to learn faster than its competitors."

The eight companies featured in this book have demonstrated the growth characteristics that today's investors are looking for and that today's companies need to emulate. The companies hail from diverse industries and regions. It should be noted that many of them are A.T. Kearney clients. We have selected these companies not only because each expressed a willingness to tell its story, but because each has an extraordinary track record of growth.

Commitment to the customer is at the root of Singapore Airlines' success. From flying a twin-engine Airspeed Consul between Singapore, Kuala Lumpur, Ipoh, and Penang to boasting the world's most modern fleet and a route that spans more than 90 cities, SIA has risen to the top of its field in less than three decades. A maverick airline from its beginning in 1972, SIA refused to join the powerful International Air Transport Association, a cartel that the fledgling airline deemed too restrictive. Instead, SIA set its own standards and has since become the world's sixth most profitable airline, one that is frequently cited as the best carrier for customer service.

Bristol-Myers Squibb is a powerhouse in both the pharmaceuticals industry and in the business world as a whole. At the end of 1998, BMS's market value exceeded $133 billion, and it ranked in the top 15 of publicly traded companies worldwide in terms of market value. But in the early 1990s, two particular challenges — the expiration of a critical patent, with no replacement in the pipeline, as well as increasing governmental pressures — had forced BMS to find a new growth strategy to carry it into the future. By focusing on productivity, BMS effectively redesigned the company, improving processes and reducing costs across the board.

Braun got its start in the roaring twenties, when Max Braun set up an appliance shop in Germany. Since then, an unwavering commitment to developing superior products, creating innovative designs, and, most important, to achieving customer satisfaction has led Braun's remarkable growth. Today, Braun makes about 200 different products, with a daily output of more than 150,000 units.

In 1928, Motorola opened its doors with just five employees, a weekly payroll of $63, $565 in cash, $750 in tools, and — the critical element — a design for a battery eliminator. Since then, the company has enjoyed unparalleled success in the world of technology. From car radios to two-way radios to semiconductors, Motorola has become a company that creates its own future, rather than waiting for the future to happen. Vision and constant innovation have driven Motorola's phenomenal growth, and the company now ranks number 34 on the Fortune 500 and employs 133,000 people — a far cry from opening day more than 70 years ago.

Australia's Carlton and United Breweries experienced a topsy-turvy roller-coaster ride to reach its current leadership position. In 1983 CUB was at the top of its game. As a new acquisition of Elders IXL, it was the leader in the Australian beer market and enjoyed almost half of total market share Down Under. But through a series of market and corporate changes, business dipped. By 1991 CUB recorded a serious loss, and its long-term future seemed grim. A change in leadership brought the necessary changes to help CUB climb back to the top. Over the past 5 years, CUB has recorded an average profit increase of approximately 15% a year and stands as Australia's number one brewer, with a frothy 56% market share.

In contrast, South Korea's SK Telecom stands as a model for hypergrowth — a straight-line, fast, and furious climb to the top. In 1993 the 9-year-old company risked everything by adopting an experimental, untested digital technology called CDMA. By May 1998, just 5 years later, the number of subscribers topped 5 million, and just 10 months after that, the total broke 7 million. These numbers become even more impressive considering that they were achieved amid the Asian economic crisis.

Bertelsmann also serves as an excellent example of continued growth. Based in Germany, the Bertelsmann group began as a publishing house in 1835, and now runs multimedia businesses around the world, including more than 300 companies in 50 countries. Its sales in 1998 reached $13.5 billion, a nearly 15% increase over the previous year. Bertelsmann's growth over the past 50 years largely rested with its ability not just to adapt to an industry, but rather to help define it. The company's innovative approach to bookselling led it to create and then dominate the mail-order book-club business. But the market has not stood still. Today, Bertelsmann continues to build on its tradition of cutting-edge growth by taking a lead position in e-business. In 1998 it purchased controlling stock in Barnes & Noble and invested in barnesandnoble.com, one of the world's largest electronic retailers.

One of the most remarkable and history-rich stories told here is that of the Singapore Port Authority. In 1819 the port retained its first commissioned harbormaster and established itself as the gateway to Southeast Asia. Left in near ruins at the end of World War II, it has since grown into one of the biggest and most reliable container ports in the world. Since 1964, when it took an enormous risk to become a container-based terminal, it has enjoyed a compound average revenue growth of more than 10%.

Separately, the story of each company tells a unique tale of growth. Together, they symbolize the type of sustainable growth that many companies want — and need — to emulate. There are no guarantees of future success. Unlike the children's story, there is no goose to lay a golden egg. Nonetheless, as each chapter reveals, these companies have found their own paths to achieve successful and sustainable growth. For the future, they can look not only to their own past, but also to the pasts of others like them. And for those companies just starting out, or even for those that may need to get back on track, we hope this book will offer insight and lessons that may help them achieve that elusive fairy-tale rise to success.

CASE 1

SINGAPORE AIRLINES

By

Christopher Clarke

Singapore Airlines

FLIES AGAINST THE ODDS

Although Singapore Airlines may annoy its long-established, more powerful rivals with its maverick ways, it knows how to please consumers. By thumbing its nose at standard airline practices and committing itself to customer service, Singapore Airlines managed to overcome the fact that its home base was not a strong one: a tiny nation with few natural resources. Now the sixth most profitable airline in the world, Singapore Airlines avoids complacency by pursuing continuous improvement. Its latest initiative is to build on its established strengths in customer service by creating a powerful network of alliances. Equipped with a revolutionary model for customer service and newly established alliances with other carriers, Singapore Airlines stands ready to raise the stakes yet again in a highly competitive industry.

OPEN SKIES OVER SINGAPORE

Singapore Airlines (SIA) was formed in 1972, after the Republic of Singapore's independence from the Malaysian Federation and the ensuing breakup of Malaysia-Singapore Airlines. At a time when most countries viewed their national airlines as expressions of state pride, Singapore recognized the hopelessness of building a successful airline based primarily on serving a population of 2 million. Consequently, the new government, which owns more than 50% of SIA, favored an open-skies policy — a rare attitude in the then heavily protected and regulated global airline industry. This policy forced SIA to compete against long-established, powerful rivals, many of which had the benefit of large, protected domestic markets.

To succeed in these competitive skies, the airline developed a distinctive vision: SIA would offer superior customer service and would achieve its growth through a customer-oriented culture. As part of its emphasis on customer service, SIA adopted an exceptionally bold stance. It refused to join the powerful International Air Transport Association (IATA), a cartel with an overabundance of rules, regulations, and restrictions (one of which even prescribed the thickness of an airline sandwich). Staying independent of IATA enabled SIA to deliver superior customer service by providing free beverages and headsets in economy class long before these amenities became standard. This maverick approach infuriated some competitors, who tried to insist that SIA conform to prevailing industry standards. One executive from a large European state airline scolded: "You are a small airline from a small country. Start behaving accordingly!"

Michael J. N. Tan, an executive vice president with 38 years of experience at the airline, remembers: "There was a vision to develop SIA into a unique airline offering the highest quality of service in the business. But who in the world was going to believe that a fledgling airline from a country with no natural resources and a small local market could measure up? This did not deter us." The airline moved quickly to implement its plan. The first step was to develop a business strategy that addressed customer service. SIA recognized that superior customer service comes from two basic sources: "hardware" (including top-notch aircraft and maintenance) and "peopleware" (such as customer-focused processes and business culture).

HARDWARE FOR CUSTOMER SATISFACTION

Singapore Airlines' market analysis showed that passengers take safety for granted and regard it as an absolute essential of airline travel. After safety, customers rank cabin and seat comfort and reliability of flight schedules as their most important concerns. SIA decided that the only way to meet those important customer expectations was by having the most modern fleet. The company ordered two new Boeing 747s — the best jets on the market at the time. This was a daring financial move for a young company that lacked the passengers to fill the planes. The airline realized that it needed world-class maintenance, not only to keep aircraft efficient, cabins clean, and schedules reliable, but also to increase profitability and efficiency. In the long term, buying the best planes and keeping them in top condition would result in higher aircraft availability, greater fuel efficiency, and lower expenditures on maintenance. This, in turn, would generate funds for further investment and growth.

However, buying and maintaining the latest planes were only two aspects of SIA's strategy, as illustrated in Figure 1. The cycle of buying superior aircraft and maintaining them in world-class condition leads to exceptional customer service and satisfaction. Thus, the integration of a number of functions to create a favorable business system generates excellent profitability and funds for further investment.

SIA's early investment in huge 747s was merely the first step to keep pressure on itself by buying aircraft and scheduling flights ahead of demand. Since then, scheduling more flights at new times has become part of the company's core competency in customer service. Figure 2 illustrates how offering more flights creates greater customer choice, which, combined with high customer satisfaction, wins market share.

Ensuring underlying demand to keep flights full supports profitable growth. When SIA scheduled more than one flight a day from Europe, competitors were skeptical, just as they were when it broke from tradition to offer daytime flights from Europe. In fact, the initial daytime flights were so successful that additional daytime flights were scheduled and have also become profitable.

PEOPLEWARE: ATTENTIVE AND INNOVATIVE CABIN SERVICE

From the beginning, SIA developed strong capabilities in cabin service and customer handling on the ground. In the air, it offered such innovations as superior food, free drinks in economy class (contrary to IATA regulations), and highly attentive service. Behind these innovations lay a finely tuned process of conducting market research, generating new ideas, and training cabin crew in new service offerings.

SIA advertisements featuring the Singapore Girl emphasized not only the cabin staff's welcoming smiles and neat appearance, but also their willingness to serve. Today, the company maintains a highly selective recruitment program and conducts rigorous training and retraining that builds a powerful service culture, including strong peer pressure to meet all in-flight and other service standards. SIA's service culture is essential to its success in customer service. Even if

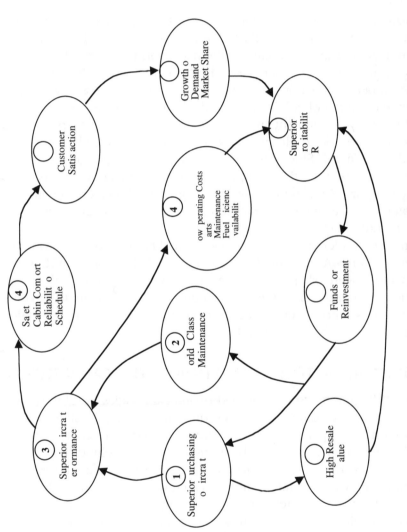

Figure 1 Integrated Capabilities at SIA.

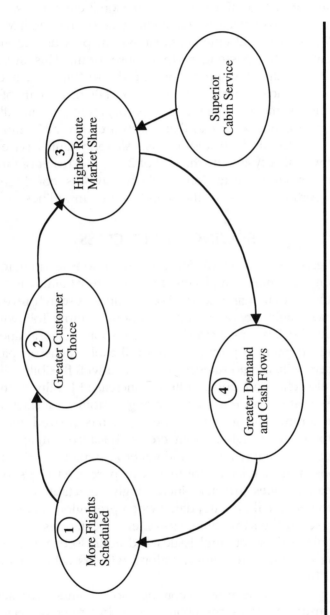

Figure 2   Scheduling Competency for Growth.

competitors copied SIA's training manuals, they would still be unable to replicate the level of service SIA is able to achieve.

SIA was the first to offer interactive personal entertainment systems in all classes of travel, via a system it jointly developed with Matsushita. The KrisWorld personal entertainment system provides 22 video and audio channels for passengers to choose from. This system now achieves 99.8% reliability and has produced a 10% increase in customer satisfaction on those aircraft where it is installed. As part of its continuous improvement program, SIA is beginning to install a new Wiseman entertainment system that boasts a choice of 25 movie titles, 50 short features, and 50 audio CDs. All long-haul service will be equipped with this system by the end of 2000. The result of this intense focus on customer satisfaction is clear: travelers consistently rank Singapore Airlines as one of the world's best run airlines.

STAYING WORLD CLASS

Despite these positive reviews, SIA uses continuous learning to prevent its staff from becoming complacent. Rigorous crew training is constantly updated to meet changing needs. For example, research revealed that cabin crews might be perceived as robotic, simply following long, memorized checklists of instructions. In response, the airline revised its training program to promote a more flexible focus on passengers as customers. When rigid rules were replaced with flexibility, the staff's priorities also changed, and resulted in increased loyalty to the airline and an associated concern with ensuring customer satisfaction.

As the airline has grown, however, it has proved increasingly difficult to recruit suitable cabin crews. Because Singapore's labor force tends to be highly literate and generously paid, workers hesitate to take jobs in the service sector that some perceive to be subservient. Singaporean families are also increasingly reluctant to allow their children to become flight attendants when prestigious alternative jobs are available. At the same time, customer expectations are rising. SIA has recognized these cultural issues and addressed this dilemma by expanding employee recruitment along with its schedules in Indonesia and India.

Customer service is now becoming more competitive across the airline industry. As SIA's competitors have lost their protected status and subsidies, they have been forced to improve customer amenities. SIA has responded by continuing to raise the bar. Sometimes it does so in spite of its own research. For example, research has shown that meal quality is not high on the list of customer needs, yet Singapore Airlines now offers world-class gourmet food and drink. The airline believes that the "need" for gourmet airline cuisine is similar to that of the Sony Walkman: once it is available, customers will prefer the new option even though they did not previously perceive a need for it. The airline recognized the limitations of its own expertise in food and has brought in an advisory panel of seven international experts to help develop menus. It also works with food suppliers to deliver the best cuisine. The food offerings now differ according to cultural or national tastes on different routes, and signature dishes have been created under the banner "World Gourmet Cuisine." Singapore Airlines again raised the competitive bar by offering free champagne in economy class on long-haul flights.

THE NEW MODEL

Perhaps one of the most significant developments in customer service is SIA's new model, shown in the table that follows. The customer is now viewed as a guest, not a passenger. In recognition of this shift, the airline is passing control to the customer. KrisWorld was a first step in that direction, and audio-video on demand and meals on demand are further steps.

Old Model: Focus on the Passenger	New Model: Focus on the Guest
1. The customer is a passenger traveling from A to B, to be made comfortable, adequately fed, and offered entertainment.	1. The customer is a guest in our cabin who is entitled to on-demand access to food, entertainment, and other services.
2. Customers are handled en masse. "It's feeding time, wake up!"	2. The customer is an individual with personal timing and service needs, and is empowered to schedule services to match his or her needs.
3. Airlines schedule service to a set timetable that suits their system.	3. We organize around the customer, not vice versa.

SIA expects its new customer-service paradigm to lead to the introduction of yet more new cabin technologies that will allow customers further freedom of choice and timing; and the airline plans to support customers by providing unique personal services at individual times.

NEW CHALLENGES AND NEW COMPETENCIES

SIA has responded to the Asian economic crisis by placing greater emphasis on its lucrative long-haul sector. Originally SIA established its stronghold by exploiting Singapore's strategic location in the days when planes had to stop and refuel in Southeast Asia. Those days are gone. To continue to attract traffic to its hub, SIA is promoting Singapore as a stopover through a promotion called "Singapore Splendor." This program offers the first hotel night for only $1 (U.S.), with discounts on meals, shopping, and tourist attractions.

To defend its position against the threat of no-frills, low-cost competition, SIA has also introduced a second, "fighting brand" — Silk Air — a medium-priced airline in terms of meal quality and seating space. Silk Air has been successful in limiting competitors' entry into SIA's home turf in Southeast Asia. SIA feeds traffic to Silk Air and vice versa. This approach is being copied by other airlines elsewhere. SIA's flight scheduling emphasizes integration of long-haul and regional services for both SIA and Silk Air.

As global competition increases, all airlines are offering more direct services. This is a potential threat to Singapore's hub position. In response, SIA has formed alliances designed to reduce its reliance on Singapore's Changi Airport. The alliances provide integrated destination-to-destination ticketing and bind customers to the alliance members' schedules. SIA sees this as a key area for its strategic growth and has already forged alliances and code-sharing agreements with Lufthansa and Scandinavian Airlines (both of which are members of Star Alliance, the world's premier airline alliance).

As costs in Singapore continue to rise, SIA is maintaining its growth and creating alliances by investing abroad. It is focusing on Asia, where growth rates are higher and costs are lower than in Europe and North America. Asian investments also offer the synergy of regional feeder services. Thanks to its prudent fiscal policies, SIA has the capital to cement alliances by taking stakes in other airlines, as it did in Taiwan's China Airlines. To meet its target of earning 15% of profits from overseas, SIA has also established joint ventures in China, India, and Vietnam. Although the economic crisis has dampened the firm's economic growth in the past year, the airline has outperformed its competitors and expects profits to begin.

The astonishing growth of Singapore Airlines is a good example of what Harvard Professor Michael Porter has observed in other companies and industries: by overcoming local disadvantages, firms become powerful competitors.* The airline developed a commitment to customer service, risk taking, and continuous improvement, which enabled it not merely to survive, but to thrive in the global marketplace.

The future looks bright for SIA. From its modest beginnings in 1972, with a fleet of only 10 aircraft and service to 22 cities in 18 countries, it now boasts the world's most modern fleet and serves 90 cities in more than 40 countries. Truly, SIA's growth has been phenomenal. SIA's strategy — to ignore the rules and compete with the best airlines in the world, no matter what the obstacles — has reaped many rewards. In the words of CEO Cheong Choong Kong, "Competing with the best made us what we are today."

ABOUT THE AUTHOR

Christopher Clarke is a vice president at A.T. Kearney. His consulting specialties include strategy, restructuring, mergers and acquisitions, divestment, and corporate finance. He is based in Singapore. In addition to his A.T. Kearney experience, Mr. Clarke served as a managing director of Wallace Smith, an investment bank in London, from 1985–1991, and earlier, as a consultant for Deloitte, Haskins & Sells, also in London.

---

* Michael Porter, *The Competitive Advantages of Nations* (Free Press: New York), 1980.

CASE 2

BRISTOL-MYERS SQUIBB

By

Doug Tunnell

Bristol-Myers Squibb

THE PRODUCTIVITY ADVANTAGE

Bristol-Myers Squibb (BMS) is known to the world for its pharmaceutical products, and it will also be known to the business world for its unconventional yet remarkably successful growth strategies. Despite cries from Wall Street for the company to slash costs in the early 1990s, BMS executives stood firm in their financial commitment to R&D and instead embarked on a transformation that not only reduced costs, but served to reignite the firm's growth engine.

THE WALL STREET WARNING

In the early 1990s, the entire pharmaceutical industry faced grave profit pressure. U.S. health-care reform initiatives sponsored by the Clinton administration seemed to be paving the way toward nationalized health care. Throughout the world, governments struggling with rapidly increasing healthcare costs demanded across-the-board price cuts, threatened to delist noncomplying drugs, and instituted promotional taxes.

Even compared to other pharmaceutical companies, Bristol-Myers Squibb (BMS) was in a difficult position. The patent for its most important product, the cardiovascular drug Capoten, which was responsible for 15 to 20% of the firm's total profitability, was about to expire. Unfortunately, no single successor with comparable "blockbuster" potential existed in the pipeline.

This fact was not lost on Wall Street, which was already looking at pharmaceuticals with new eyes. The financial analysts knew that the days of high gross margins and annual growth rates in the mid-teens were over for the industry as a whole. They also believed that there was only one thing for a company in BMS's position to do: slash costs and put more money on the bottom line. The strategy the analysts recommended, both to managers and in print, boiled down to "milking the business."

Management, led by chairman Charles A. Heimbold Jr., disagreed. BMS had always been a "value" company, achieving steady growth in earnings and delivering solid, stable, blue chip returns to shareholders. The company was committed not just to maintaining profitability, but to creating maximum value for shareholders over the long term. BMS refused to mortgage its future for the sake of near-term earnings, and instead looked to develop a model to achieve continued growth and success in the new business environment. The firm also needed to convince Wall Street that BMS was not just a value company, but a growth company. As CFO Mike Mee put it, "There was a need to demonstrate that we were a growth company, and that we were not going to save our way to prosperity."

To grow revenues and profits while preserving dividends, BMS needed to free up funds and invest in two things:

- *Research and Development.* A refocused and energized R&D function would bring more attractive products through the pipeline faster.
- *Marketing.* Stronger marketing capabilities would carry BMS's messages about its products — those in production and those to come — both to the right set of prescribing doctors and to a public that had recently become accessible to direct pharmaceutical advertising.

One way to free up funds would have been to follow the analysts' advice and, for example, cut 10% of costs across the board. That would have given BMS the short-term results managers sought. But they reasoned that doing so might lead to cutting essential costs and paralyzing the organization. Moreover, there might be areas where 30% cuts would make more sense, and areas where no cuts were appropriate.

BMS chose another strategy instead, one based more on building than on dismantling. The strategy was to overlay a new key competence upon those areas on which BMS had traditionally relied: R&D capability and sales and marketing strength. That new competence was productivity. As the past few years have proved, by making productivity a core competence, BMS has achieved new levels of innovation, created an organization that gets maximum mileage from every dollar it spends, and improved returns despite a hostile environment. Productivity is now integral to everything the firm does. Today, Wall Street is convinced that BMS has a future as a growth stock, and share price has increased roughly 400% since the end of 1994.

DEFINING PRODUCTIVITY

At BMS, productivity is not simply targeted cost cutting. Rather, productivity means, in effect, redesigning the company from scratch to develop processes that work better and often cost less. Thus, a process that needed 50 people might be redesigned to require only 20 people, but the 60% cost cut would be accepted only if the new process worked at least as well as the old one.

In fact, many of the new processes resulted in no lost jobs. More often they involved a shift of decision making that took advantage of scale economies wherever they made most sense. Thus, productivity, in many cases, meant enhanced leverage of existing resources.

These improvements frequently were driven by technological improvements. The company placed heavy emphasis on finding ways technology could make it more efficient. This led to new processes with substantial technology components.

Managers began to think differently about "what matters" in the business. They identified huge savings opportunities in areas that had previously been organizational backwaters, but those savings would be available only if those sectors of the organization were managed by skilled and savvy people with enough clout to make things happen. Without an enterprisewide productivity lens, for example, who would have envisioned that purchasing could make major contributions to the bottom line?

Not only is the BMS productivity effort still in place, it helps tie the company together because by now it has affected virtually every part of the organization. People throughout the company are measured and motivated in terms of productivity. Decisions in manufacturing, R&D, and sales and marketing are evaluated against the question, "Will this make our group as efficient and effective as possible?" What began as "a catalyst for change" has become an integral part of the corporate culture. BMS is now full of believers in productivity. However, no change process as far-reaching as this is ever smooth.

SETTING THE TARGET

From the outset, it was clear that productivity could be improved substantially in the short term by eliminating the redundancies remaining from the Bristol-Myers/Squibb merger of 1989. The question was, how much more improvement could be found? There was considerable debate as to whether the target should be made public. Some believed that if BMS published a specific number, the program would be viewed as complete once the goals were reached. Others pointed out that if the number was big enough to make BMS a growth company, it might be a "freezing event" that would paralyze people whose only thought would be "here come job cuts." Some managers also suggested that setting a target would set artificial limits for the firm.

Still others countered that the firm needed a public objective for three reasons: to build credibility; to create a measurable goal; and to put management at risk, both internally and in relation to Wall Street. In short, naming a figure would keep BMS honest. It would also provide a wake-up call to the organization, which, until that time, had paid more attention to performance against budget than performance against competitors. With this internal perspective, managers tended to see "no burning platform," despite the concerns of Wall Street analysts.

In the end, executives decided to establish objectives. They targeted to achieve $1.1 to $1.5 billion in productivity benefits by 1998, with "productivity benefits" defined as a combination of gains used to fund incremental spending on R&D and sales and marketing, and improved earnings performance.

Clearly, this was a stretch target that could not be achieved through savings alone; something fundamental had to change in the organization. Fortunately, the message was received and acted upon. In fact, BMS met the initial productivity targets and new, more aggressive goals have already been set.

LAUNCHING "PRODUCTIVITY FOR GROWTH"

The idea of productivity was not new to BMS. Before the merger, the Squibb organization had had a culture of productivity that was built into MBOs and recognized by the chairman at award dinners, although productivity was viewed in terms of individual projects rather than an enterprisewide concern. At Bristol-Myers, the manufacturing function had always had a traditional productivity focus based on measuring inputs and outputs at the microprocess level.

More recently, some critical work in R&D led to a new model. Early in 1994 that business unit had set itself the task of becoming more productive. Ken Weg, head of the pharmaceutical business, defined productivity in terms of reducing development time. The project reduced the time from PLP (preclinical lead profile) to IND (investigational new drug), which had been 20 months on average at BMS at the beginning of this initiative, to an average of 8 months. While productivity work in other parts of the company would be aimed at freeing up funds rather than doing things faster, managers knew that many of the approaches used in the R&D work could be taken elsewhere, specifically:

■ Assignment of a project team with a dedicated leader, supported by part-time team members
■ Use of outside consultants where appropriate
■ Careful use of metrics to set benchmarks and targets
■ Rapid implementation of team suggestions and measurement of results

The next step was to apply these guidelines to the entire company. To do this, BMS launched the Productivity for Growth program, which consisted of a broad range of productivity initiatives that maintained profitability at a critical time while enabling incremental investment in R&D, the sales organization, and marketing. The linkage with investment in growth has been critical to the success of the productivity effort. In fact, it was only when this was understood and believed that the initiative gained broad buy-in and support across the company.

This program tackled both manufacturing and G&A (general and administrative) areas from a global perspective, that included Ken Weg's pharmaceutical business plus the consumer and medical devices businesses, both of which reported to Mike Autera.

Top management believed that the level of strategic commitment needed to be demonstrated organizationally, and began by forming a very visible Productivity Steering Committee (PSC) at the top of the company. Mike Autera was named chairman at the committee's formation in the summer of 1994. Mike Mee succeeded him in this capacity in the fall of 1995. The members, who included Ken Weg and Michael Mee, all committed half their time to the project for the first 6 months. Doug Tunnell (this author) was added as a senior vice president out of the strategic planning function and made the committee's project manager.

The committee had a busy 6 months, aimed at getting the productivity initiative off to a very visible and very well-informed start. All the committee members went to the operations, meeting with managers to say that productivity was important and to listen and probe for best practices and opportunities to make the company more productive. But the top-level commitment to productivity was for more than 6 months. All the members knew that, after some time, the committee might meet less often, but it must continue to exist and oversee BMS's permanent commitment to productivity. The PSC exists today and is still made up of direct reports to the chairman, although it meets much less frequently.

The PSC identified specific initiatives, or streams of work, where members felt productivity improvements were achievable:

- Purchasing and distribution
- Companywide processes
- Shared services
- Asset management
- Information management
- Manufacturing network
- Facilities and real estate
- Segment selling
- Supply chain

For each initiative, a high-profile team was formed that was headed by a full-time individual taken from a vice-president or director-level position for the purpose. This use of *A-Players* sent a strong signal. So did the fact that the team leaders came from outside the function; this ensured a fresh look at the function and a healthy suspicion of "sacred cows." Everyone understood that this effort involved risk, so incentives were used liberally to create an upside that would encourage the right people to lead and staff the teams. In fact, the first layer of bonus was awarded "just for showing up," with an additional incentive attached to results.

As expected, the Productivity for Growth program yielded quick hits in cost savings as well as critical lessons for the whole organization about leadership, culture, and efficiency. Two examples of these initiatives are improving purchasing power and centralizing shared services.

Purchasing Power

One of the earliest productivity efforts, and one of the most powerful, was aimed at the purchasing function. Led by Rick Nabb, the team included representatives from plants around the United States and outside consultants who helped the team "think out of the box" and provided training in methodology. The team began by identifying categories of expenses that appeared to offer substantial cost savings. At the time BMS was spending twice as much on indirect expenses, such as temporary help and travel, as it did on costs of goods or direct expenses, so the team looked at both categories.

The team worked to understand the driving factors in each market and to use that knowledge — combined with the buying power of BMS — to structure a series of arrangements with suppliers that would pull money out of the relationships. In many cases this involved consolidating suppliers, which was possible even for goods and services that had to be provided locally.

For example, one direct cost was corrugated cardboard. Because of the cost of freight, a corrugated plant can supply material cost effectively only within 200 miles, and based on that understanding, BMS plant managers had been buying from a total of 35 vendors, sometimes at the individual plant level. BMS had never approached the market with the buying power of the $15 billion corporation that it was. But when it did, it quickly became apparent that national makers of corrugated cardboard with multiple locations exist, and these manufacturers were willing to offer a price based on BMS's total usage. The same proved to be true for a key indirect cost: temporary help. Again, national players could price a high-volume national contract very attractively, while still supplying a location-constrained resource.

The fact that many such opportunities existed showed that purchasing had not previously been viewed strategically at BMS. It also showed that for many expense categories, specifically those that are used similarly across geographies and have the same level of strategic importance, it makes sense to centralize purchasing activity in order to show one face to the market. Nabb's team negotiated numerous contracts at the national level, saving upwards of $100 million in the first year (1996) alone.

These results were not easy to achieve. Although no jobs were cut by the procurement effort, some local managers strongly resisted their loss of power — both to choose their own suppliers and to benefit from the deals they struck locally. Once the purchasing team had negotiated a contract, it informed the local managers that, henceforth, they should order a material or service from a particular supplier; that the national contract would save X dollars; and that, therefore, the local budget would be cut by the same amount. Naturally there was pushback. Nabb describes his role during that time as "human punching bag." A number of local managers simply did not comply, and after about 18 months, the project stalled.

At this point, leadership from the top was needed to reinvigorate the effort — and it came. Rebellious managers received personal visits from Mike Autera, who explained that the organization was serious about productivity and that cooperation was needed. Importantly, at the same time, top management transformed Rick Nabb's project team into a global purchasing organization, with the resources to not only negotiate contracts but also to enforce compliance. Soon afterward, the results of the national and global contracts began to appear on the bottom line. Predictably, as the productivity effort demonstrated more and more success, it gained more and more supporters.

With a stronger mandate, the group began to "think the unthinkable," that is, to examine make-vs.-buy trade-offs in areas that had previously been "too hot to handle." One such area was facilities management, where for a time the team considered outsourcing 1400 maintenance jobs. They decided not to, after facilities managers made commitments to reduce their costs substantially and become competitive. No other activities have been outsourced to date, but the possibility remains open.

Once an organizational backwater, procurement is now a key contributor to BMS's bottom line. Beginning with the savings of over $100 million in 1996, the purchasing organization has achieved results that any function can be proud of: savings of $450 million in 1997, $700 million in 1998, and an estimated $850 million in 1999.

This project underscored the importance of the principles of the productivity effort:

- The need for active, visible senior management support throughout a culture-changing experience
- The need to invest and dedicate enough high-quality people and other resources to ensure that such an initiative is done well
- The need to demonstrate enough early wins, or "quick hits," to prove that the culture shift has a real reward
- The need for a good governance model to enforce the change

One issue was still up in the air: when was the best time to introduce an organizational solution? Nabb's team had begun as a task force. Only after 18 months, after it had proven its value and demonstrated its need for formal organizational clout, did the task force become a formal headquarters function, with a budget and dedicated staff. Would an earlier organizational solution have gotten the job done faster or better? That question was addressed by the shared-services project described below.

Centralizing Shared Services

From the top-management perspective, nothing could make more sense than centralizing back-room operations, or "shared services." The routine processing of financial transactions, such as accounts payable and invoicing, is not critical to individual businesses, and centralization would yield economies of scale. Beyond the cost savings, this would send a strong message. As Mike Autera said, "We were taking routine, noncritical activities out of the divisions so that the business units could focus on what makes money for the company. This highlighted the fact that we were operating as one company, not a group of autonomous divisions." Therefore, BMS centralized routine financial transaction processing in a group called financial shared services.

In retrospect, it would be tough to find a more difficult initiative. In the purchasing work, quick financial wins had proved the wisdom of centralization and the organization change followed logically. In this case, BMS led with organizational change, and the financial results were slow in coming.

Having centralized shared services, it made sense to centralize the technology that would support it. SAP was an obvious, rational way to approach an enterprisewide piece of software. The result was not only the largest single instance of an SAP implementation in the world, but probably one of the most successful SAP implementations ever completed.

The team started by calculating the theoretical optimal benefit that would come from implementing SAP. To realize that benefit, BMS needed to have standardized financial reporting systems and, ultimately, manufacturing systems across the company. This would mean, of course, rationalizing the remaining, separate Bristol-Myers and Squibb systems. The team decided to back off commonality only as an absolute last resort.

SAP was implemented first in the financial shared services organization, and it was clear that the centralization had been necessary; if the reporting had been left in the divisions, there would always have been reasons why standardization was impossible. The pharmaceutical business in central New Jersey was the first group to be serviced by that organization, and the system has been rolled out to the operating units. Today, BMS's SAP development and implementation are centralized and cost effective.

The return has been impressive, but it was a long time coming. The organizational solution was needed in this case and proved valuable, in that it sent a strong signal about how the company would work henceforth. However, it was a painful process, partly because it had to be an act of faith.

The team took a key lesson away from this experience: if you are going to tackle the organization, understand why you are doing it and be confident that it makes a lot of sense. You want to do it only if there is a compelling reason.

MOVING AHEAD WITH PRODUCTIVITY FOR GROWTH

As BMS moved ahead with other Productivity for Growth projects over the next 2 years, teams tended to avoid organizational solutions. Partly, this was because every step they took away from basic transaction processing was a step closer to the core of what is unique about the individual business units. For example, an ethical pharmaceutical business and a consumer business (such as BMS's Clairol division) have very different distribution requirements, and their distribution networks need to be designed differently. The early productivity work convinced the team that if there are good strategic reasons for not changing the organization, it should be left alone.

The other initiatives bore fruit in terms of increased productivity as well. Two examples are

- The manufacturing network initiative achieved significant savings by analyzing global capacity requirements and streamlining manufacturing through plant consolidation. The total number of pharmaceutical plants worldwide was reduced by more than half.
- The facilities initiative put in place plans to cut millions of dollars in costs through the implementation of hundreds of savings ideas in areas such as maintenance, grounds keeping, laundry, utilities, and food and mail services.

MAKING SALES AND MARKETING MORE PRODUCTIVE

By late 1996, there was increased awareness of the need to enhance the effectiveness of the sales and marketing functions of the pharmaceutical business. It was clear there was an opportunity to apply the lessons learned about productivity elsewhere in the company. In particular, management had come to understand that increasing productivity involves a common commitment to best practices, and that this may require relinquishing some individual freedom. So the sales and marketing efforts, which were global in scope, moved some power from the country managers' hands toward the center. As in the R&D work, team leader Myrtle Potter focused on metrics as the basis for change.

After looking at the pharmaceutical sales force, Potter's team concluded that the single most important factor determining sales-force effectiveness was the number of days representatives spent in the field visiting target doctors. They found great variations in this metric across countries. The team developed new global definitions of the roles of representatives and managers. The definitions included metrics defining the optimum number of days a representative should be in the field, and the optimum number of calls to be made to targeted physicians. Country managers then received higher sales targets that were based on a more effective and productive sales force, along with a set of recommendations and metrics for reducing the nonsales commitments of the sales force.

Potter's work in marketing addressed the key interactions across the business from product development to commercialization, and focused in particular on marketing planning and product launch. From a global perspective, she knew that a coordinated launch would best leverage global marketing assets and investment in drug development while maximizing the market's attention on BMS's new products. The result, again, was a reduction in local power for the sake of enterprisewide best practice.

COLLABORATING ACROSS FUNCTIONS

As productivity permeated BMS, management began to think further out of the box. New skills and knowledge are now shared across functions and, as a result, productivity synergies are emerging in unexpected places. Here are three examples:

Making Science Commercial

The Marketing Effectiveness team, led by Myrtle Potter, could mandate a global launch by working within marketing alone, but to shorten the time to global launch, it had to work more closely with the drug development group. Historically, the marketing effort had begun as soon as the drug was approved for launch. To get a running start, marketing now works with development during the development process itself, and the early marketing work is done in parallel with the final development effort. Potter believes that bringing a commercial perspective to development has another key benefit: it allows the marketing department to help decide whether there is a market for the drug being developed and what indications would have the most potential. "Instead of science that was sexy, we wanted science that was commercial," Potter explains.

The revamped development cycle builds in inputs from marketing and go/no-go decisions based on commercial considerations. This has led to the earlier shutdown of projects with low commercial potential, freeing up more resources for the projects most likely to contribute substantially to BMS's bottom line. In essence, the cross-functional cooperation has made both development and marketing more productive.

Procuring Clinical Trials

A second example of cross-fertilization is the application of a procurement principle — that of aggregating demand and negotiating based on volume — to the area of clinical trials. Rick Nabb's sourcing organization used BMS's size to cut development time while guaranteeing the high quality this function demands. They approached a select group of clinical testing houses and offered them partnership arrangements in which BMS receives preferred treatment, and a guarantee that the testing organization will always test BMS drugs with its A-team. In exchange, the research firm gets a major client and a look at what's coming down the pipeline, which allows it to staff, hire, and recruit accordingly.

BMS development managers are not required to use these preferred suppliers, but they usually do. Nabb's team chose preferred suppliers known to deliver excellent quality. Quality was assured since the providers had promised that BMS projects would be done the right way, by their best people. The R&D group felt no loss of autonomy.

Procuring Market Research

In a similar effort, procurement techniques were used to economize on United States market research. BMS was buying market research across the company, but had always done it by division. Nabb's procurement organization worked closely with marketing people around the country to evaluate all the existing market research contracts, pull together a preferred supplier list, and negotiate contracts. This early communication with stakeholders won acceptance for the program, and the savings were substantial.

THE BOTTOM LINE

The financial markets have observed and rewarded the positive impact of BMS's productivity efforts. Having come from behind, BMS has, since 1994, outperformed the S&P 500 and seen its price-to-earnings ratio triple and its market value more than quadruple.

Today, BMS lives and breathes productivity. New processes allow more to be accomplished with fewer resources while permitting investments in growth. The numbers tell the story. Despite the expiration of the Capoten patent and the impact of the mix shift to lower-margin products, the company has maintained its margins, even while investing significantly in the growth of the business.

The choice to add productivity to BMS's traditional set of core competencies sent shock waves through the company, but the shock was healthy. Indeed, BMS is better positioned for the demanding 21st century than competitors that have relied solely on the traditional pharmaceutical strengths of R&D and sales and marketing excellence.

ABOUT THE AUTHOR

Doug Tunnell, a University of Texas graduate in business, joined E.R. Squibb as International Assistant Controller nearly 20 years ago, and is currently senior vice president, Global Business Services, of Bristol-Myers Squibb. He is a member of the company's Productivity Steering Committee and led the implementation of the BMS restructuring effort. Mr. Tunnell is responsible for the corporatewide SAP implementation effort, the corporate financial shared service centers in the United States and Europe, the Worldwide Strategic Sourcing Group and the worldwide infrastructure function, including communications, hardware, desktop support, and applications development for the Worldwide Medicines Group.

CASE 3

BRAUN

By

Archie Livis and Dieter Rams

Braun's Mission

TO MARRY TECHNOLOGY AND DESIGN

The story of the Braun Group illustrates how combining functional design with innovative technologies can redefine the rules of competition in both traditional markets and new ones. By offering superior products and being flexible enough to drop once successful lines that are no longer profitable, Braun has kept a quality compact with customers. Braun's distinctive designs and technological advances have helped turn a German producer of small appliances into a global company with operations in eight countries that generate more than $1.7 billion in sales annually.

LEADER IN INNOVATION

Braun AG, a unit of the Boston-based Gillette Company, is known as much for design as for the products that it sells. But it remains a company firmly focused on its 200 small appliance products. Its 9000 employees turn out more than 150,000 individual items a day in eight countries, including Germany (where 65% of its products are still made), Ireland, France, Spain, Mexico, China, India, and the United States.

Braun is the world sales leader in foil shavers, cosmetic depilatory devices, plaque removers, hand blenders, and infrared thermometers. Currently, the company's most successful product innovations include the Flex Integral razor, the Braun Oral-B Ultra Plak Control plaque remover, the Supervolume Twist hair dryer, the Silk-épil Body System device for cosmetic hair removal, and Multiquick hand mixers. But more than its products, the Braun name is synonymous with design.

It has not always been that way. In 1951, when Artur and Erwin Braun inherited control of the company owned by their father, Max Braun, product design was handled by design engineers, similar to other firms and typical of business at the time. But within 2 years, the two sons moved product design to center stage. They redesigned a line of phonographs and radios and brought fresh designs to the firm's Multimix food processing machine and its hallmark product, the electric razor.

To make aesthetics a selling tool, in 1954 the Braun brothers brought in Professor Wilhelm Wagenfeld and several of his associates of the School of Design in Ulm. The result was a unique and much admired "Braun Design." This new and creative approach to design, combined with Braun's emphasis on innovation, quality, and customer satisfaction, pushes sales to new highs.

The shift to focus on design was not a superficial or halfhearted attempt to differentiate the company, but a top-down desire to offer products that would be more useful and more in tune with people's needs than the products offered by competitors. Although the introduction of advanced designs carried the risk of losing consumer acceptance, the gamble of paying more attention to aesthetics proved successful — and not only with consumers. Leading designers have repeatedly praised Braun for innovative concepts and awarded the company a wide array of international prizes. Braun appliances have even found their way into a collection of the best contemporary products at New York's Museum of Modern Art.

Although Braun's designs serve to make its products distinctive on store shelves, the design philosophy remains centered on the customer. Braun believes that functionally designed products can enhance and improve the user's life. Design must continuously improve a product's useful characteristics — handling, ease of use, and durability. Designs are also shaped to promote efficient production and adoption of modern manufacturing techniques and new materials to cut waste and conserve natural resources.

As always, a good idea quickly attracts competition, and Braun's introduction of bold new designs brought challenges from larger consumer product organizations on both sides of the Atlantic, including Bosch, Siemens, General Electric, and Philips. However, unable to match either Braun's superior products and superior design, competitors failed to capture Braun's lead position as a design house. For example, one of Braun's products, the Sixtant razor, stood both the test of time and competition. Introduced in 1962, the new razor's technically superior foil was smoother, more efficient, and less irritating to the skin. Product managers had determined that the razor would be both technically and aesthetically innovative. The Braun Sixtant did not look like previous razors — its matte black style made it stand out from all of the shiny silver razors on the shelf. Marketed as a "high-performance instrument for men," the Braun Sixtant proved to be an unusual and enduring commercial success.

As the Sixtant illustrates, a vital component of the brand image that Braun has built over the decades is the superior functional benefit of its products. This functional image gives Braun a competitive advantage and effectively differentiates its brand from competitors'. Today, because competitors can often quickly introduce new products to supersede the usefulness of existing products, brand image is increasingly important.

Fritz Eicher, Braun's design and engineering chief, once noted that Braun products are "conceived for intelligent people who have a feeling for authenticity and quality, whose living space is simple, practical, even comfortable. Our appliances should fit in and look the part. They are not products made for the shop window which attract notice by being particularly obtrusive, but rather appliances with which one can live for a longer period of time."*

A DESIGN BEYOND FUNCTION

With an eye always on its customers, Braun has continuously developed and strengthened its proficiency in design and technology, and has focused on the development, manufacturing, and marketing of quality products with innovative technology and functionally oriented design.

The design competence at Braun is based on a clear concept. Product designers consider themselves "creative engineers" — technically oriented designers. They take notice of the development of cultural values in human society and integrate these values into their designs.

While good design is the creed, the mission of the company's creative designers is continuous product development. Products introduced

---

* Hartmut Stroth, Erfolg durch Qualität. Die Braun Multisystem Story, in Brigitte Wolf, ed., *Design-Management in der Industrie* (Giesen, 1994), p. 148.

within the past 5 years account for 70% of company sales. That means that the company relies on a constant pipeline of new product offerings. To bring these new offerings onto the market as quickly as possible, Braun spends significant amounts on product development and production optimization. Constant in-house testing reveals ways to improve existing technology; and everyone participates. To test a razor, for instance, Braun asks employees to shave under controlled conditions and to report back on the product's ease of use and feel.

Consistent high standards of quality have been essential to the company's growth and success. Fulfilling customer needs worldwide requires complete order transparency, 24-hour service, and delivery in exact accordance with customer specifications. Zero-defect production is standard, and internal controls ensure that each group's work meets company expectations.

Braun's focus on research and development does not always mean abandoning old products for new, however. Braun's popular food processor was produced for 35 years almost without change. Braun simply saw no need to change it. The product performed well and enjoyed strong sales. A new food processor was introduced only when it became apparent that the updated version would add measurably higher value.

Braun's impressive growth can also be attributed to its willingness to leave a market if it can no longer meet its own high standards. Braun exited the audio products market in the 1970s when it determined that it could no longer supply "Braun quality" at a price that could compete with imports flooding in from Asia. Even though its products had sold well for decades and were highly respected for their quality and innovation, Braun saw that it was time to leave. Ever mindful of its loyal customers, the company took the highly unorthodox step of informing customers that it was leaving the market through a new line called Last Edition. The line was meant to appeal to experts and collectors of Braun devices, and was accompanied by an attractive history of Braun audio design. Braun provided a 3-year guarantee and promised that spare parts would be available for 10 years. The Last Edition proved to be an impressive sales success.

THE MISSING LINK

Braun's emphasis on quality reaches into the minute details of production and logistic processes. Research and development, strategic product marketing, and critical manufacturing processes are all located in Europe. Braun believes that the high cost of German labor is offset by superior job performance. The company relies on its employees' expertise to support its technologically advanced production processes.

Braun also manufactures in Mexico and China, where it makes razors powered by rechargeable batteries. However, the parts that are crucial to the performance and quality of the devices — the shaving heads — are manufactured in Germany and assembled in Shanghai.

WINNING WITH THE UNIQUE EDGE

For every Braun appliance, technology, design, and marketing worked together to create clear and convincing benefits that users can easily recognize and remember. For example, based on dental research, Braun introduced the plaque remover, an entirely new personal hygiene appliance. The device has been clinically tested and is recommended by dentists worldwide.

Braun will continue to rely on its unique combination of technology and design to offer greater customer benefit than its competitors and achieve new levels of growth. In the short term, it is unlikely that any other company in the industry will be able to overtake the competitive advantage Braun has created.

▼▲▼

Design for Vision and Company Philosophy

During Braun's early years, product designers developed and shared the company's philosophy as they searched for the optimal solution. Only later did the organization draft a written set of guidelines for design. Those guidelines are intended merely to stimulate thinking; they are neither comprehensive nor obligatory. In essence, they emphasize that Braun strives for designs that make appliances optimally useful and show the greatest care for even the smallest detail. They promote timeless designs that have nothing to do with trendy styling. According to the guidelines, good design is

- *Innovative.* Good design neither repeats known product designs nor generates innovation for its own sake. Rather, it is innovative only when such innovation will significantly improve a product's functions.

- *Practical.* The customers who buy a product intend to use it. The product should thus perform specific functions, both primary and ancillary. The primary task of design is to optimize a product's usefulness.
- *Aesthetically pleasing.* A product's aesthetic quality must be integral to its usefulness. Trying to use a product that is not well designed can be confusing and annoying; using a poorly designed razor can be a literal pain in the neck.
- *Easy to understand.* Good design clearly illustrates a product's purpose and is essentially a product's voice. A successful design makes the product self-explanatory and eliminates the need to read instructions to learn how to use the product.
- *Unobtrusive.* A product that fulfills a function is a tool. It is neither a decoration nor a work of art. Its design should be neutral, to allow the appliance itself to recede in importance and leave room for users to enjoy its full benefit.
- *Honest.* A product should not appear to be something it is not. Design should not manipulate buyers and users, nor should it incite them to self-deception.
- *Durable.* Good design is not trendy and should not quickly become outdated.
- *Consistent to the last detail.* Care and exactness in design express respect for the product and its functions, as well as for the user.
- *Environmentally friendly.* Design can and must contribute to the protection of resources. Well-designed products are durable, guard against pollution and perform in ways that maintain the environment.
- *As little design as possible.* Back to the pure and simple!

═══════════════▲▼▲═══════════════

ABOUT THE AUTHORS

Archie Livis is Braun's executive vice president, Chairman's Office, Global Business Management Division, Diversified Group. In this capacity, he has worldwide responsibility for all research and development, manufacturing, and strategic marketing for Braun personal care and household appliances and stationary products. Mr. Livis joined the Gillette Company's Canadian subsidiary in 1959. In 1984, Mr. Livis was named to the Board of Management.

Dieter Rams is an architect, interior designer, and industrial designer. In 1955, Mr. Rams joined Braun AG as architect and interior designer. In 1961 he became chief designer and in 1968 became the director of the product design department. He led the product design team to develop a new corporate image for the company and a new generation of electrical appliances, including shavers, food processors, audio equipment, and cameras. Mr. Rams is a professor at the Hochschule für Bildende Künste in Hamburg, Germany. He is also the honorary president of Rat für Formgebung, the German council for design.

CASE 4

MOTOROLA

By

Eike Bär

Motorola

WHERE R&D CREATES NEW INDUSTRIES

Motorola is a company that values technological innovation. In fact, it has invented products that have spawned entirely new industries. It has thrived by consistently envisioning the need for a new product and then developing the expertise and infrastructure to meet that need. What is more, the company has a history of listening to — and even advocating — ideas contrary to the official corporate viewpoint. Motorola gives internal dissenters a formal opportunity to present their views and their supporting evidence. The organization believes that such sessions highlight weaknesses that might otherwise be overlooked because of groupthink or organizational enthusiasm for the corporate plan.

VISION TO REALITY: A RETROSPECTIVE LOOK

Clearly thought-out visions and the single-minded determination to realize them have driven Motorola's success since the company was founded in 1928. Initially, visions were born from the inspiration of the company's entrepreneurial leaders: Paul Galvin, Motorola's founder, and Bob, his son and the company's longtime CEO. The Galvins translated their ideas into innovative and successful products that drove the company's growth and became ubiquitous in the United States marketplace and, later, throughout the world.

As the company grew, the Galvins realized they needed more corporate visionaries and inventors to maintain the momentum. Thus,

Motorola introduced processes and tools that would institutionalize innovation and enable a much broader group of managers and associates to develop new ideas.

The results are now things of legend: Motorola's inventions — the car radio, the portable two-way radio, and the semiconductor — rewrote the competitive rules in numerous industries and marked Motorola as a company that creates its own future rather than waiting for the future to happen. Today, technological expertise still forms the basis for Motorola's global leadership in its core sectors of mobile communication and semiconductors, and continues to drive its phenomenal growth.

DETROIT NEVER HEARD IT COMING: THE CAR RADIO

At the dawn of the wireless communication era in the 1920s, Paul Galvin had a plan to combine two brand new technologies: the radio and the automobile. Galvin reasoned that the time and inevitable boredom involved in driving long distances might stimulate demand for a new product: the car radio. He believed that mobile communication would be of increasing importance to society, especially for commercial and security purposes.

To support Galvin's vision, Motorola worked to develop specific competencies in radio-frequency technology and interference-free electrical and mechanical technology. It needed to master these capabilities to develop a radio with the mobility to operate in a changing climate, the robustness to cope with fluctuations in temperature and atmospheric conditions, and the endurance to transmit both speech and music with quality and clarity.

"MISSION CONTROL, THIS IS APOLLO CALLING"

In the mid-1930s, Paul Galvin had a new idea. A decade of prohibition had led to the rise of organized crime, which was rampant in Chicago, Galvin's hometown. Galvin realized that if the police were to respond effectively, they needed to be constantly linked to an operations center, even while in their patrol cars. He combined a mobile radio receiver with a mobile radio transmitter to create the two-way radio.

And just in time. As World War II escalated, the first portable radio, the walkie-talkie, was developed. Military demand pushed this product into volume production, and another new industry was launched. Of course, people who use radios for security require greater reliability and robustness and demand smaller equipment than do users of simple car radios. Thus, the Motorola engineers found themselves challenged to build upon the expertise they had gained through the development of car radios to meet the exacting demands of their new customer group.

The experience served them well. In the 1960s, Motorola radios were to prove their worth under even more extreme conditions, as part of the Apollo space program. Neil Armstrong kept in touch with Mission Control from the moon via Motorola two-way radios in his backpack. The astronauts who followed him used Motorola radio equipment in the moon buggy. Developing such equipment provided yet another opportunity for Motorola's engineering team to broaden and deepen competencies acquired back on Earth.

SEMICONDUCTORS: A RADIO JOINS CORPORATE AMERICA

Motorola started to develop semiconductors shortly after the invention of the transistor in the 1950s. Once again, a Motorola executive with strong technical skills created a new industry and proceeded at his own risk to turn vision into reality. The company reasoned that a radio-like device, in addition to serving a broad range of security purposes, might lead to productivity gains in the industrial and service sectors. Combining semiconductor technology with radio expertise enabled engineers to make significant improvements in durability and size, which were just as significant as reductions in power consumption. Motorola's continuously advancing semiconductor expertise allows the company to sell the smallest cellular phone available today and to supply the world's largest car manufacturers with Motorola chips to control engine functions.

AN INCUBATOR FOR NEW BUSINESS

In the 1980s, Motorola drove new wireless communications markets, including paging and cellular telephony, but technology alone was not enough. Motorola was also a pioneer in globalization; it acquired international expertise in spectrum availability and radio frequency economies, two areas that proved to be of crucial importance to future growth.

Today, the company's operations are directly related to its earlier innovations because its earlier products continue to find new markets. Examples include products in the following fields:

- *Professional radio technology.* As markets in Eastern Europe and Africa have opened, this technology has proved that the deregulation and liberalization of wireless communication can carry economic benefits.
- *Person-to-person communication.* At a time when most providers of telecommunications service dismissed the "car phone" as a toy for millionaires and pseudo-sophisticates, Motorola invested considerable sums to develop and market a portable cellular phone. It was suddenly possible to talk to people on the go.

Motorola even gained a bonus when developing countries, which did not have telecommunications technology, leapfrogged from wire to wireless and became huge new markets for Motorola's cellular phones and other wireless technology.

- *Paging.* Paging, a spin-off of radio technology, was born from the union of semiconductor technology and wireless receiver technology. Further innovations, such as combining numbers with alphanumeric displays, using vibration to create a silent ring, and offering creative approaches to billing, allowed sales of this device to grow to billions of dollars.
- *Wireless data for a mobile workforce.* To overcome the limitations of two-way voice-based data transmission, Motorola developed innovative data radio equipment and systems for specific applications, including United Parcel Service's e-based system. The Motorola system provides this leading small-package deliverer — and its customers — with the real-time location of each package in the delivery chain.

Motorola incubated the new strategic business units within its Communications Sector until their market potential was firmly established and they could be spun off into separate businesses. This approach proved beneficial because the internal competition between the new and core businesses tended to stimulate them both. In addition, as the new business incubated within the existing one, it both motivated the development of new ideas and ensured that the existing business base would not be neglected in favor of the new one.

RENEWAL AT THE CORE

In the course of Motorola's long history, its Land Mobile Products Sector became an internationally recognized supplier of professional radios and radio systems. One measure of its success was the constantly growing market share that its products enjoyed in most areas. Less apparent, but just as critical to its marketplace strength, was the company's direct sales and customer service organization. By maintaining close contacts with end users and pursuing an ambitious research and development program, Motorola identified emerging consumer needs and translated them into improved or new products, but growth could not continue forever. Although the organization continued to enter new geographic markets, the inevitable happened: as the penetration level of the core professional users increased, growth slowed and return on investment shrank. It was time for a fresh vision to identify who the next users of mobile radio technology could be.

By the late 1980s, Motorola's Land Mobile Products Sector was oriented toward professional users: police and fire departments, medical emergency units, utilities, and the gas and oil industry, among others. Such users had demanding product requirements that constantly challenged the capabilities of Motorola's development and manufacturing units. Motorola had long been aware of another potential market: private citizens' band and amateur radio users. However, because those users did not need many of the features required by the high-end professional users, Motorola largely ignored them.

That was not the case with a number of Asian manufacturers, who moved into what they perceived to be an underserved market. By improving productivity and response speed, but ignoring high-end features and services that their target users did not want to pay for, the Asian manufacturers quickly captured the market. To keep costs down, they marketed their new equipment through indirect channels, without direct sales forces. Motorola recognized this competitive threat only after the new vendors were well entrenched in North America and Europe. At corporate headquarters in Schaumburg, Illinois, top managers called for an immediate response.

Motorola could not become a leader in the new segment simply by marketing cheaper versions of its existing professional radio line. Only when Motorola formed a new team, charged to act independently and to compete with its existing businesses, did it achieve its corporate goal of conquering the new market segment. The company debuted an entirely different, limited product line under the brand name Radius, which it sold exclusively through indirect channels to a targeted group of end users. Motorola learned and applied new organizational and marketing capabilities to meet the requirements of its new customer base and trade partners. These included new ordering procedures, logistics arrangements, sales promotion, trade management, and discount policies.

TWO KIDS, TWO CARS, AND TWO-WAY RADIOS

As Motorola continued to expand its radio business, it researched the barriers to the adoption of mobile two-way voice and data communication by a much broader group of end users. In addition to equipment-specific features such as price, size, weight, and ease of use, one previously underestimated barrier was identified: restrictions imposed by the telecommunications regulatory authorities. At the time, many jurisdictions granted licenses to a very tightly defined group of end users, including public authorities, utilities, and emergency services. In Germany, for example, the application process was time-consuming, expensive, and complex, especially when the user wanted coverage in all German states. An expensive monthly license fee further reduced the radio's attractiveness.

Nevertheless, because the Radius product line had proved so successful, Motorola decided to develop easy-to-use, low-end radios for previously unserved end-user groups. The company believed that tradespeople and contractors, and even sports enthusiasts, were all potential users of low-cost two-way communication.

Eventually, licensing authorities granted the radio industry frequencies to serve those needs in major countries worldwide. The licensing procedure was streamlined or, in many countries, eliminated altogether. This helped Motorola realize its vision of serving new users with radios that were developed specifically for their limited requirements, represented good value for the money, and required a minimum of regulatory red tape. This concept has proved very successful in pilot markets. The early results suggest that it may eventually be possible to make two-way radio communication available to every family in the industrialized world.

MAKING POSSIBLE "WHAT YOU NEVER THOUGHT POSSIBLE"

The Land Mobile Products Sector was only one of many Motorola businesses that underwent renewal in the 1980s. The financial results for the corporation are worth noting: a 15% compound annual growth rate over 25 years as revenues climbed from $800 million in 1970 to more than $27 billion in 1995. Until the late 1970s, a few visionaries in top management drove the process of renewal.

However, over the past 15 years, the growth enjoyed both globally and in innovative markets could not have been achieved without the participation of a much broader group of managers. Eventually, Motorola addressed the challenge of how to teach the entire organization to create visions, recognize those visions, and capitalize on them.

▼▲▼

From Toolkit to Innovation

Motorola's approach has been to develop tools to drive the company toward learning and innovation. It developed some of its methods internally and adapted some from other companies' best practices or by working with the proponents of new ideas. Motorola promotes the continuous testing of new management ideas and hones those practices that have demonstrated success. The organization uses three tools, each designed to address a different time frame, to help management take a long-term perspective, envision a successful future, and, as Motorola says, make possible what you never thought possible.

1. *A roadmap for technology.* Twice a year, every business unit presents its Technology Roadmap to top Motorola executives. At this forum, key managers hold detailed discussions of technology strategies for the next 10 years. Each roadmap is a synthesis of the opinions of many experts — from both inside and outside the company — and reflects their understanding of relevant technological trends and how demographic, social, political, and organizational changes may affect the markets on which Motorola depends.

   A key component of the roadmap is the minority report, in which dissenters to the strategy formally present their views and their supporting evidence. The company has found that allowing — even promoting — dissension often reveals weaknesses that, in the general enthusiasm for the plan, might otherwise be overlooked.

2. *Strategy at the center.* Motorola conducts an annual Strategy Center with a totally different purpose: to translate the ongoing

vision into the actions necessary for realization over a 5-year period. Strategies are developed to enable every department to achieve ambitious growth and profit targets. These strategies result from an intensive analytical process to which most functional areas in the business contribute and upon which management may set certain conditions. The strategies focus on potential sources of growth and improved competitive position.

Senior managers often use sections of the Strategy Center document to communicate strategic objectives throughout the organization. They also review the action plans quarterly to ensure that forward momentum is maintained. The most important aspect of the process is not the document itself, but rather the subtle effect the process has on managerial thinking and the setting of priorities throughout the entire organization. This process, and an internal timetable that is strictly adhered to, ensure that thinking about the future is not put off until competition is knocking at the door.

3. *Scenario options.* Unlike the Technology Roadmap and Strategy Center processes, which are both based on intensive analyses and follow strict timetables, Scenario Option Development is a fluid process that Motorola uses every 2 or 3 years to evaluate complex and uncertain developments. Scenario Planning not only can help the organization challenge the inevitable sacred cows that arise in corporate groupthink, but also can identify trends before the usual indicators reveal a shift. During Scenario Option Development, managers work together to develop a joint understanding of the external environment in which their business operates, and the ways in which it might change.

The process forces managers to imagine and respond to extreme, polarized possibilities and to assess their potential impact on their business. What actions should the organization take to succeed in each possible future environment? How can managers "future-proof" the organization so that changing circumstances will not force them into making hasty adjustments that could be too little and too late?

Technology Roadmaps, Strategy Centers, and Scenario Option Development are parts of a toolkit that Motorola uses to build on existing capabilities, create new visions, and develop new growth strategies. But tools are not enough. Inventing new industries requires commitment as well as vision. The tools are a structured method of tapping into the expertise that already exists within the organization and galvanizing the company to act promptly on the resulting information. The payoff is a future-proof and successful global organization. At Motorola, vision and commitment keep the entrepreneurial spirit of the Galvins alive and ensure solid growth and increased returns on shareholder value.

ABOUT THE AUTHOR

Eike Bär is the managing director of Motorola GmbH, and corporate vice president. He is also general manager for the company's commercial, government, and industrial solutions sector responsible for Europe, Africa, and the Middle East. He has been with Motorola since 1981. Mr. Bär holds an M.B.A. and a masters degree in mechanical engineering from the Technical University of Berlin.

CASE 5

CARLTON UNITED BREWERIES

By

Nuno D'Aquino

Carlton United Breweries

VISION FOR LEADERSHIP DOWN UNDER

Carlton and United Breweries (CUB) is Foster's Brewing Group's largest subsidiary and its core domestic Australian business. Over the past 5 years, CUB has recorded an average profit increase of approximately 15% per year, expanded its share of the Australian beer market from 48 to 56%, and launched a series of innovative products and new lines of business in the hotel and leisure market. However, CUB's performance has not always been so impressive. Not so long ago, buffeted by changes in its market, economic reversals, and strategic miscalculations, CUB was in danger of losing its preeminence. It took a new CEO with a new vision to pull the company out of the doldrums and establish it as a lead enterprise. Newly invigorated, CUB has made the extensive changes in strategy, operations, and culture that will ensure its ability to continue its strong growth trajectory and lead Australian industry into the future.

BEER MAKING DOWN UNDER

In 1983, the Australian food conglomerate Elders IXL acquired Carlton and United Breweries in a reverse takeover and, as a result, became one of Australia's largest companies. At that time, CUB was the leader in the Australian beer market, with almost one half of total market share. It was also highly vertically integrated, and owned maltings and hop farms, carton and bottle factories, in addition to extensive hotel and retail interests.

The purchase of CUB marked the beginning of Elders' strategy to grow by acquisition. CUB became Elders' cash cow for funding its ambitious growth program, which included investments in agriculture, mining, and mineral businesses. Elders also sought to establish Foster's as a global brand by investing in brewing operations in Canada and the United Kingdom. During this period, Elders significantly reduced its investment in CUB and sold most of CUB's noncore activities. When the stock market crashed in 1987, Elders' diversification program ground to a halt and the company reversed its direction from growth to consolidation.

The bad news continued. By 1992, Elders (now called the Foster's Brewing Group) had recorded a loss of $1 billion (Australian), which led to extensive corporate restructuring and increased emphasis on reducing costs and consolidating operations. To ensure its own survival, CUB renewed its concentration on its core business. It closed several breweries, sold or leased back property, slimmed down its hotel business, and cut back capital expenditures for technology.

At the same time, the beer market also underwent significant changes. The Australian brewing industry had essentially evolved into a duopoly, as the two major national players, CUB and Lion Nathan, acquired or increased their holdings in the few remaining independent regional breweries. Meanwhile, beer consumption steadily declined as consumers began to turn to wine and lighter drinks. As a result, liquor store chains emerged as an increasingly powerful purchasing group.

Faced with these changes and with serious declines in market share and profit that threatened its preeminent market position, CUB executives realized they were not addressing the requirements of most Australian consumers and that the company's long-term prospects were bleak. CUB's leaders needed to refocus and create a new vision of how it could move forward and continue to grow.

VISION: A FRAMEWORK FOR DEFINING SUCCESS

The new leaders began the reinvention process by developing a fresh vision that was less specific to selling beer but gave greater attention to all the elements required to be a world-class organization. CUB determined to change its focus from "being the market leader in beer" to "becoming a lead enterprise whose practices, products, technology, and financial performance would be recognized as among the world's best by its peers." CUB's lead-enterprise vision was based on the following two fundamental beliefs:

- An organization's only sustainable competitive advantage is its ability to learn faster than its competitors.
- There is no such thing as a mature business.

These two beliefs guided CUB as it changed its strategy, operation, and organizational culture to achieve its vision of becoming a lead enterprise and rejuvenate its growth.

The company formed a 15-person cross-functional, cross-hierarchical team to define what it would take to become a lead enterprise. The team decided the best way to describe the company they wanted to become would be to illustrate how then-current CUB practices needed to change. For 12 months, various subcommittees drafted the changes required for CUB to become a lead enterprise and developed a list of competencies required for all staff and work teams to put the new concepts into practice.

A VISION FOR LEADERSHIP

The lead-enterprise vision spurred a profound strategic shift at CUB. The model challenged the company to continuously review its business and refine its understanding of both the existing capabilities it needed to expand and the new capabilities it needed to acquire.

For a start, if CUB hoped to grow significantly, it needed to change its business proposition. The company could no longer afford to view end users (in this case, beer drinkers) as its only customers. CUB needed to continue to satisfy the tastes and needs of beer drinkers, but it also needed to focus on its various retail channels and recognize them as valued customers as well.

In essence, CUB was changing from a "brewer" to a "high-value beverage company," and was changing its primary purpose from manufacturing and selling to managing the value chain. It took the organization approximately 18 months to fully understand the implications and opportunities associated with this shift. The company used

Table 1   Concept Shifts at Carlton and United Breweries

From Beer Company	To High-Value Beverage Company
Our strategic decision making will be guided by	
Manufacturing and selling	Managing the value chain
Management of resources	Knowledge exploitation
High-volume production	Mass customization
Ad hoc product development	Strategic innovation
Our organization structure will be based on	
Department, individual focus	Networked cross-functional teams
Sales organzation by state	Distribution channel focus
Our day-to-day management will be characterized by	
Ambiguity	Clarity of purpose
Task focused	Project driven
Production driven	Customer focused
Managing	Leading
Championing individual differences	Think nationally, act locally
Our view about people	
People as workers	Workers as people
Our goals and objectives will be achieved through	
Unidentified capabilities	Leveraged core competencies
Market demand leading technical development	Technical research — a catalyst to change

Table 1 to explain the strategic implications of the plan and the areas of capability required to achieve it.

BENEATH THE FOAM

The concept shifts that CUB instituted at the strategic, operational, and cultural levels continuously guide the company's growth. CUB regularly reviews its competitive position to assess and redefine the competitive advantage it aims to create. This process has identified specific capabilities the organization needs to develop, maintain, or reinforce to pursue particular growth opportunities. The following examples illustrate the elements of CUB's new vision.

Brand development

Many of CUB's capabilities to support its core beer business are standard in the industry. Because a brewery can expect a very short lead time whenever it introduces a new product, CUB needed to enhance its core production and marketing capabilities. CUB also invested in the following three areas to support its development of new products:

- Consumer research, to develop a deep understanding of consumer tastes and changing requirements.
- Brewing technology, to create a more flexible system to support mass customization.
- Corporate structure, to form adaptable teams able to work in parallel on development tasks.

As a result, CUB's new product launches have been highly successful. In fact, CUB now leads in areas where it had been caught off guard by new competition in the early 1990s. CUB recently launched a series of new brands targeted at distinctive, unexploited segments of Australia's beer market:

> *Carlton Cold*: The first cold-filtered beer in Australia, and the first clear-glass mainstream beer to target the 18- to 30-year-old market.
> *Foster's Light Ice*: The first clear-glass, midneck beer in the light segment. (The brand is driven by an image of refreshment using active sports vs. traditional taste messages.)
> *Carlton Mid Strength*: A full-tasting beer in the midstrength category that uses a double-hopped brewing technique to deliver a more satisfying flavor.
> *Premium Dry*: Premium-tasting dry beer in an embossed long-neck bottle to capture the growing subpremium category.

Perhaps more significantly, CUB has been able to establish a leading position in the category of alcoholic sodas with its Sub-Zero brand. This product combined the company's capabilities in biotechnology and brewing technology with its understanding of consumers and image creation. CUB successfully brought a more sophisticated edge to the new-age beverage market, where it now enjoys a 60% share.

Retail

Brand-owned pubs and hotels have traditionally been part of a brewer's distribution operations in Australia. Until a few years ago, CUB viewed its pubs and hotel retail outlets as distribution channels rather than as businesses in their own right. CUB did not think about running pubs and hotels as a core competency and, in 1993, even considered leaving the market. Two factors led CUB to take a second look: the growth of gaming in Australia (thanks to the liberalization of poker-machine laws) and the internal changes produced by its new vision. Consequently, executives conducted an internal review of operations, which led them to think that they could incorporate CUB's hotel and pub investments into the growth strategy.

The review highlighted several gaps, but it also indicated important capabilities the company could use to improve its hotel and pub business. Since then, CUB's market research and marketing capabilities have helped the hotel business outperform the competition in discerning its customers' needs. This improved understanding of the market has fueled the development of new restaurant concepts. The retail business has moved away from the traditionally dark spaces that focused on alcohol consumption to more family-oriented venues that offer gaming, food, and light entertainment as well as beer.

The company developed targeted service concepts aimed at maximizing the opportunities of a locale by extending the function of its space. For example, CUB's franchised sports bars, *Sneakers*, have space for pool tables, TV and music videos, and horse-race betting, in addition to the bar. The lighting, music, and activities in each of these venues change during the day to enhance the mood of the room.

Another example is the dining business. Here CUB has developed three different service concepts: "AYCE," a self-service, all-you-can-eat format; "Beacon's," a limited-service dining format with a children's play area; and the full-service "Davy's."

This brand concept not only gives customers a better sense of their dining options, it also gives staff at each restaurant a framework for assessing critical parts of the business and improving attention to detail and customer service. In addition, this business approach served to highlight critical capability gaps in food management and menu design, which the organization has since worked hard to fill. CUB has also leveraged its brand by creating *Liquor Express*, a chain of liquor shops associated with the pubs.

By systematically capitalizing on its capabilities in market research, branding, and professional management, CUB has significantly improved the profits of its retail business (see Figure 1) and developed an impressive chain of retail establishments. Indeed, the company now has such confidence in its retail business that it recently announced the acquisition of a new chain of pubs and hotels, making it Australia's largest operator in the industry.

The profitability decline in 1998 and 1999 (see F98* and F99* in Figure 1) is due to the acquisition of over 100 hotels, which have low operating margins. CUB, however, is confident that it can raise the performance of the acquired hotels to the group average, and so reverse the profitability decline it has experienced since 1998.

The lead-enterprise vision guided this remarkable growth by encouraging the organization to focus actively on developing solutions, rather than viewing changing demographics and trends as potential obstacles.

Logistics

The lead-enterprise vision emphasizes management of the supply chain. CUB conducted a strategic review of industry best practices, which led it to completely reconfigure its own approach to logistics. The organization integrated its supply chain, from raw material suppliers to retailers, including purchasing, planning, and delivery. For example, CUB now uses sales forecasts to drive raw material requirements, production, and production sourcing.

The short-term benefits include less warehousing and improved lead times, which in turn result in higher customer satisfaction. In the longer term, CUB expects to increase revenue by further developing its logistics capability to cover vendor-managed inventories and e-business activities.

Change Management

CUB is experienced at managing organizational change. Even before the new vision led CUB to reinvent its business, its change-management capability was highly successful. The emphasis on cost cutting in the early 1990s provided the catalyst for this development. At that time, much of the company's workforce was underskilled and bound to a craft-based industrial culture that impeded the sharing of knowledge and slowed the company's response time to market demands. Key

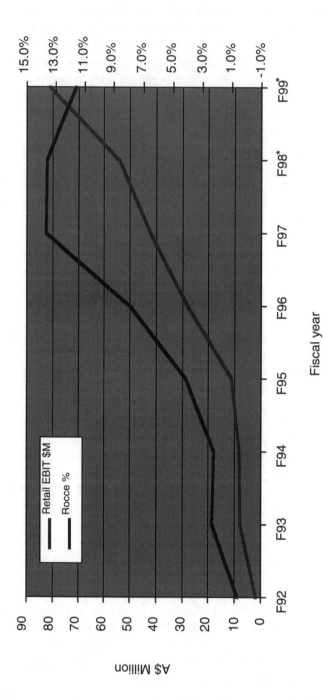

Figure 1 Retail Performance.

concepts such as "self-organized work teams" and "leading by learning" have since been put into practice throughout the organization and have sped the organization's response to change, and thus its ability to grow.

New information technology systems have also played a key role in helping CUB manage change. The IT systems are designed to expedite and encourage strong horizontal communication and to replace the traditional approach of communicating up one functional silo and down the next.

Carlton and United Breweries' key strengths in managing change lie in the following three areas:

- Adopting an evolutionary, yet aggressive, approach to change that is based on a detailed understanding of the organization's past, with an eye toward future growth
- Applying a consistent set of values at the individual, team, and companywide levels that are reinforced by performance measurement and incentive programs
- Understanding how to manage the balance between today's bottom line and a program for change that will affect tomorrow's financials

HALF EMPTY OR HALF FULL?

CUB is proud of the financial returns the lead-enterprise vision has brought so far (see Figure 2). However, the journey has just begun. E-business, changes in logistics, and the fragmentation of consumer demands are already bringing new challenges as the company grows. Nevertheless, thanks to its lead-enterprise vision, CUB is better positioned now than at any time during the past 10 years to actively lead Australian industries to meet those challenges.

ABOUT THE AUTHOR

Nuno D'Aquino initially joined Carlton and United Breweries as a laboratory technician in 1961. He has held numerous positions with the company and ultimately, in 1994, was appointed to his current role of managing director of CUB. Under his leadership, the company has gained an international reputation for technical excellence. Mr. D'Aquino was born in Shanghai and moved with his family to Australia in 1952.

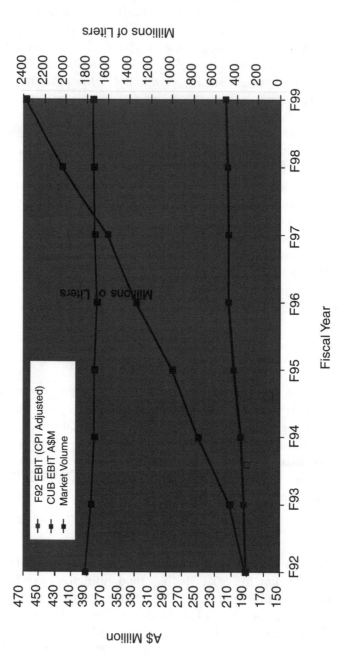

Figure 2 CUB Implementation.

CASE 6

SK TELECOM

By

Thomas Shin

Calling All Risk Takers

SK TELECOM CHOOSES UNTESTED DIGITAL TECHNOLOGY

SK Telecom, the former Korea Mobile Telecom, bet everything in April 1996, when it switched to an untested digital cellular phone system. Today the company is a new telecom giant that has helped make South Korea the fifth largest cellular phone market in the world. But, as this story reveals, SK Telecom's risk not only resulted in skyrocketing growth, but initiated fundamental changes to South Korean business practices and global technology patterns.

BETTING THE HOUSE

Six years ago, South Korea was in the early stages of transforming its recently deregulated telecom industry from analog to digital and was prepared to risk everything on an experimental, untested digital technology called CDMA. The country was hoping the United States would also be captivated by CDMA technology — lured away from the more prevalent GSM digital technology developed by European telecom carriers and fairly ubiquitous throughout Europe, Australia, Hong Kong, and other Asian countries.

If CDMA technology worked, and if the United States latched onto the CDMA star, South Korea's sole cellular provider, SK Telecom, and its emerging telecom industry would flourish. Indeed, companies would sprout up all along the supply chain to manufacture and distribute digital equipment and products, and later export their products to the United States and to other markets that were sure to follow. Alternatively, if CDMA technology failed, SK Telecom was prepared to fail with it, having wasted millions of dollars and years of effort. The decision was made. Three years later, SK Telecom became the first company in the world to offer commercial CDMA cellular service.

Looking back, South Korea's decision to take a chance on an untested, risky technology was a defining moment for SK Telecom. It led to organizational changes that vaulted the company ahead of its competitors and to improvements in one of South Korea's most tightly controlled *chaebols** — a move other chaebols would be forced to emulate following the Asian financial and economic crisis that befell the nation late in 1997. The decision also played a part in opening up a chaebol to outsiders, a first in Korean history, and in strengthening Korean exports. Exports of CDMA-based telecom equipment soared, despite the Asian crisis, going to China, the United States, Hong Kong, and the Czech Republic.

A TECHNOLOGICAL CROSSROADS

In 1993, South Korea had arrived at a technological crossroads. The country had made the decision to switch from analog to digital technology — a relatively simple decision, given that the entire world was either already digital-based or moving toward it. The problem was that digital technology offers users basically two types of technologies from which to choose.

One is GSM, which stands for Global System for Mobile. Developed by European carriers, GSM is a proven standard that works fairly well and is ubiquitous throughout Europe, Australia, Hong Kong, and other Asian countries. The other is an alternative technology called CDMA, which means Code Division for Multiple Access. On paper CDMA looks to be superior to GSM, but in 1993, it was still a new, untested technology that no other nation had committed to. The United States was leaning toward CDMA technology but was still far from making a decision, and, in fact, today continues to struggle with three different digital technologies.

---

* *Chaebols* are diversified conglomerates of many companies clustered around one holding company that tends to be family owned.

Technology Tussle

In a struggle reminiscent of the Beta vs. VHS war for the world's standard for videocassette recorders, countries and companies throughout the world are tussling over a standard for cellular telephone technology.

Essentially, the battle is over two digital technologies: GSM and CDMA. The differences in the systems are in the methods they use to convert sound into coded digital signals, which are transmitted to base stations and satellites.

CDMA proponents say their system is capable of delivering more information than GSM, offers greater security and voice clarity, and uses less power and ground area for cell sites than GSM. Backers of GSM technology refute these claims, however, and question the way the research was conducted.

GSM is the standard in Europe, freezing out CDMA, and is fairly ubiquitous throughout Australia, Hong Kong, and other Asian countries. In the United States, Pacific Bell uses GSM, while AT&T and Cellular One use a third system related to GSM called TDMA.

CDMA is in the United States (via Sprint PCS), Canada, China, South Korea, Hong Kong, and the Czech Republic. CDMA is on trial in Shanghai, Beijing, and Guangzhou in China; and commercial operation has begun in Singapore, Thailand, Indonesia, and the Philippines. (Japan uses personal digital communications, or PDC, a standard peculiar to itself.)

A phone developed for one technology cannot be used for the other, so manufacturers are being encouraged to produce phones that can receive both signals.

This left South Korea with a dilemma: go with an existing digital technology that already has numerous equipment manufacturers throughout Europe and Asia vying for market share or, alternatively, take a risk and commit to the experimental but potentially more powerful CDMA technology. If CDMA worked, South Korean companies would prosper as never before. Its local digital equipment manufacturers — Hyundai, Samsung, and LG Communications — would be able to feast on a burgeoning cellular and pager market in their own country. And later, if the United States did choose a standard, and if it chose CDMA technology as that standard, the South Korean companies would be in a position to export CDMA-based cell phones and equipment to the United States and to other countries that were sure to follow the United States' lead. After much hand-wringing, South Korea decided to take the risk and build its telecom industry around CDMA technology.

DEVELOPING STRATEGIES

SK Telecom's R&D group and engineering teams went to work perfecting CDMA technology. Its newly formed executive team worked on developing other areas (beyond cellular) that could use the technology, including satellite services, online services, and wireless cable television. The team came up with long-term strategies for marketing, customer segmentation, pricing, and distribution and developed a plan to improve engineering skills needed to compete in a digital environment, which led to programs for training and developing the workforce.

Before any of these strategies could be successful, however, the executives had to find a way to transform a stagnant, passive organizational culture. This would require an overall cultural transformation because many of the employees were still clinging to bad habits formed when the company was a government-run monopoly.* To this end, the company introduced its employees to two visions.

The first was a work-ethics vision that revolved around a program the company called "SupEx," for "SuperExcellence." The philosophy is simple. Set a goal. Set it as high as possible and then stretch it further to a point that is nearly impossible to reach. The idea is that it is better to set a goal at an unreachable 150%, where in striving to reach it you go above 100%, than to set a goal at 100% and achieve 100%. The second vision revolved around a program called "MOVE 21," in which SK Telecom set a 10-year target to reach $15 billion in revenues — a far stretch, given that at the time SK Telecom's revenues were less than $1 billion.

---

* In 1992 Korean Mobile Telecom was privatized in the wake of market deregulation and became Sunkyong or SK Telecom.

THE MARKET OPENS UP

By 1996, SK Telecom stood poised to become the first company in the world to offer commercial CDMA cellular service. It had constructed base stations and launched satellites, made necessary preparations for a competitive environment, and met all the requirements to be a force in marketing and customer service. In April, CDMA technology was launched into a market of more than 2 million cellular subscribers.

Within months, the government succumbed to international pressure to deregulate the telecom market. It was not long before a second carrier, Shinsegi Telecom, set up shop in South Korea. Owned by a consortium of 16 companies, including United States-based AirTouch and Southwestern Bell, Shinsegi was a start-up with two competitive advantages: its owners had experience in competitive markets, and its products had lower prices, part of a pricing strategy sanctioned by the South Korean government. Then, just to keep things interesting, three PCS operators entered the country's cellular market, two of which were owned by South Korea's first and second largest chaebols.

Suddenly, SK Telecom was competing with four giants, all entering telephony for the first time and investing lots of money to do so. With little experience in a competitive market and unable to compete on price, the company shifted into high gear, determining it had two major advantages over its competitors.

First, it had operational know-how in wireless telephony. SK Telecom used its experience to establish an international roaming capability to allow customers to take their phones to other countries and still call home. (All business travelers know the frustration of getting off a plane to discover an inoperable cell phone.) This was a first in South Korea and a unique customer service that none of SK Telecom's competitors could offer.

SK Telecom's second advantage was tied to its wealth of customer information. When it was a wireless carrier operator, the company had collected a database of customer information and now "owned" information on more than 12 million people, or a quarter of South Korea's population. It had a database filled with customer names and addresses, and information on customers' call patterns and spending habits.

To leverage the information, the company began using techniques in database marketing, combining SK Telecom customer data with similar information from other companies in the SK Group chaebol. Instead of focusing on market share, it began to look at its wallet share, that is, the number of sales SK Group has from any one customer.

For instance, if Mr. Kim earns $35,000 a year, what percentage of that income goes to products and services sold by the chaebol, including SK Telecom?

The strategy worked. By the end of 1997, SK Telecom had won the lion's share of cellular subscribers — nearly five million — and sales revenues had increased 31%. Local digital equipment manufacturers were prospering as never before, selling digital-based equipment to countries that had also latched onto the CDMA star.

Everything was going well, and then Asia stumbled into a financial crisis.

FELLED BY THE ASIAN FLU

A world of success cannot stop what happens to companies in an economic crisis. Late in 1997, when the bottom fell out of Asia's markets, companies and industries went under as never before. The International Monetary Fund stepped in to help South Korea with a record $58 billion bailout package, but the bailout had a few strings attached. One string was that Korea's political and business leaders had to embrace change. To meet this condition, President Kim Dae Jung persuaded the chaebol to change its parochial habits, and coaxed the militant labor unions to accept the inevitability of layoffs. Now, both the chaebol and the unions were promising to increase efficiencies and reduce staff.

However, change is difficult. The chaebol had long benefited from its closed markets, even though such protectionism had made it extremely inefficient: last year alone, Korean industries were rated at less than 50% of the United States and Japan in labor and capital productivity. The chaebol's attempts at improvement did not look promising from the outset. Union members were busy instigating demonstrations and riots opposing job cuts. In one instance, Samsung Group's endeavor to sell its construction equipment operation to Volvo sparked a demonstration that disrupted production for several days until Samsung guaranteed its workers jobs for another year.

TIMING IS EVERYTHING

For SK Telecom, the timing of the Asian financial crisis could not have been better. In fact, it turned out to be a defining moment for the company, the point at which all of its hard work would finally pay off.

Keep in mind that South Korea's decision to go with CDMA technology had forced SK Telecom to enter a competitive market long before most other Korean chaebols. Consequently, when the crisis hit 4 years later, SK Telecom was well ahead of its competitors. It had already improved its efficiency, streamlined its entire organization, and transformed its organizational culture. Now, while the other chaebols struggled to emulate these improvements, SK Telecom had two choices: it could either rest on its laurels and wait for its competitors to catch up, or improve even more and entice much-needed foreign investments.

Not surprisingly, the company decided to improve even more. One of the most popular enhancement techniques at the time was business process reengineering. SK Telecom executives wanted to avoid a full-fledged reengineering process because it would require first changing the business processes and then changing the organization to work around the new processes. They felt such a scheme would never work in South Korea, especially in a company that was once a government-run monopoly. Instead, company executives chose to work from a trigger point and first startle the organization. They decided to cut jobs.

The prospect of reducing head count forced SK Telecom to examine every level of its organization, every layer, and every person's responsibility. It called for benchmarking the top telecom companies in the world and using key performance indicators to determine how many people were really needed to operate an organization of SK Telecom's magnitude. The results showed that SK Telecom could do the same amount of work with 1200 fewer people, or a 20% reduction in staff. Soon after, 1200 people walked out the door, none through layoffs. Every person left voluntarily through an early retirement program.

SK Telecom found itself in an envious position. It had the resources to fund an early retirement program while its competitors were reeling from the financial crisis, devastated, and unable to fund anything, let alone early retirement programs. The only alternative for the other chaebols was to cut staff through layoffs, and, as mentioned earlier, union workers in South Korea were ready to do anything, including riot, to keep their jobs intact.

NEW DEMANDS TO CREATE SHAREHOLDER VALUE

SK Telecom's strong performance pushed it among the first South Korean companies targeted by foreign investors. Indeed, the Asian financial crisis opened the door just far enough for foreign investors to capture one third of SK Telecom. Tiger Management, the New York-based hedge fund, encouraged SK Telecom to give two outsiders seats on its board of directors, marking the first time in Korean history that non-Koreans would sit on the board of a company owned by a chaebol. In essence, the outsiders had purchased the right to scrutinize a Korean chaebol.

Suddenly, new board members swept in with new ideas and new demands. They called for SK Group to be more transparent in its management practices, to not invest overseas without proper due diligence, and to refrain from bolstering up other areas of the group with profits from SK Telecom. Those were typical demands for western companies, but for the chaebol, such demands were unheard of.

SK Telecom adapted. Moving quickly to satisfy its investors' many stipulations, the company launched six new improvement projects to help determine its strategic direction for the future. At its investors' request, SK Telecom backed out of a deal to ship digital mobile phone equipment to Brazil. (Although the deal appeared to be profitable, creating total exports of $400 million over 3 years, SK Telecom would have had to borrow $300 million in international capital markets.) SK Telecom also launched a $30 million manufacturing subsidiary to produce cellular telephones, marking the first time in Korea that a mobile telephone operator had its own production facility.

It is remarkable to look back and find that an earth-shattering financial crisis had so little impact on cellular phone sales in South Korea. Today, SK Telecom continues to flourish. With more than 7 million CDMA digital subscribers, plus 200,000 analog subscribers, the company is slowly migrating to digital technology. It is already moving forward in its plans to expand into "third-generation" CDMA systems, including Internet linking, faxing, and paging capability as well as crystal-clear telephone reception.

Surely, changes implemented prior to the Asian financial crisis have, in effect, helped to save SK Telecom. It is a company that mustered the courage to transform itself early on and, as a result, was able not only to survive, but to grow amid a crisis that showered havoc on countless companies and industries throughout Asia.

═══════════▼▲▼═══════════

Highlights in the History of SK Telecom

1984

- Korea Telecom, a telephone and telegraph monopoly, establishes mobile telephone service unit, Mobile Telecommunication Service Corporation of Korea.
- Mobile telephone service is available only in Seoul and its satellite cities.

1988

- Company gains independence and changes name to Korea Mobile Telecom (KMT), expanding to cover 107 cities nationwide.

1993

- KMT has 312,869 mobile telephone subscribers, up 15% from the previous year.

1994

- Korea Telecom sells 44% of KMT shares, in step with the government's plan to privatize as many government-run companies as possible.
- Sunkyong Group, a chaebol, purchases 23% of KMT shares and acquires management rights.
- Subscribers exceed 500,000.

1996

- South Korea is among the world's top 10 telecom markets with over 21 million telephone lines installed and 2.4 million cellular subscribers.
- The government introduces CDMA telecommunication service.
- South Korean government deregulates the telecoms market because of international pressure and negotiations to enter the WTO.
- Subscribers to CDMA service number 800,000.

1998

- Korean cellular phone service providers together have more than 10 million users.
- SK Telecom has 4.6 million subscribers, 80% of whom are digital phone users, making it the eighth largest carrier in the world.
- Foreign investors capture 33% of SK Telecom in March. Tiger Management, the New York-based hedge fund, insists that SK Telecom give two outsiders seats on its board of directors.
- SK Telecom investors approved its planned launch of a $30 million manufacturing subsidiary to produce cellular telephones in May.

1999

- SK Telecom has 7 million cellular subscribers, 97% of whom have digital CDMA handsets.
- Alliance with BTA of China is formed to provide "roaming service in China."
- Currently, there are discussions of wireless Internet service development and launch with Microsoft.
- Stock price has shot up more than fourfold since April 1998, from $300 to $1300.

════════════════▲▼▲════════════════

ABOUT THE AUTHOR

Thomas J. Shin is a vice president and managing director of A.T. Kearney, and he is based in the Seoul office. He has more than 10 years of consulting and industry experience focusing on infrastructure, logistics, and networking improvements in transportation, media, and telecommunications. Prior to joining A.T. Kearney, Mr. Shin served as the President of T.S.M.G. Inc., an independent advisory firm specializing in network management. Mr. Shin was previously with Goldman, Sachs & Company, where he was involved in managing various mergers and acquisitions, LBO, and IPO activities.

CASE 7

BERTELSMANN

By

Jürgen Haritz and Andrej Vizjak

Innovative Sales Approaches

POSITION BERTELSMANN FOR THE FUTURE

Today, Bertelsmann runs multimedia businesses around the world in all areas of the media market. However, Bertelsmann's success story began in Germany in the book business. By successfully combining expertise in direct mail, data mining, and standard selling techniques to develop book and media clubs, Bertelsmann has reached incredible heights in both profits and growth. Despite its size and global strength, however, the challenge is never over. Bertelsmann is now confronted with new entrepreneurial challenges, including online competitors. Bertelsmann's response to these challenges has been to systematically strengthen and develop those areas of expertise that established it as a model of growth.

BECOMING THE BEST — BY THE BOOK

When Bertelsmann entered the book-club market 50 years ago, the rules of the game did not exist; in fact, the company played a decisive role in creating them. Its innovative strategies helped make Bertelsmann a world leader in the book-club business. Every consumer who has received a direct-mail piece to join a book or record club knows how the business operates. What consumers may not know is that

Bertelsmann has been able to analyze and adapt its lists to target consumers in microspecialized niches. For example, people interested in military history are sent catalogs that cater to that interest; those interested in cooking are targeted with catalogs of cookbooks and products for the home chef.

In addition to receiving customized, preselected information about their special interests, club members enjoy substantial cost savings. Books and recordings offered by the club are typically priced at least 20% below their bookstore cost. Bertelsmann is able to do this by licensing unique editions: the club acquires a book's rights to publication and reprints it with a different cover, design, and imprint. Because the club's sales operation is enormous, it enjoys economies of scale that lead to significant savings.

The company's history began when Carl Bertelsmann opened a book printing company in Guetersloh, Germany in 1835. Its modern success, however, grew out of the ashes of World War II. When Bertelsmann reopened its doors after the war in 1948, it was a typical publishing house that distributed its books through bookstores. However, when Bertelsmann decided to step outside these traditional channels, the innovative approaches it pursued helped it to achieve stellar growth. These methods included:

- *Establishing dedicated "Bertelsmann areas" in stores.* Within bookshops, the company established separate areas where only Bertelsmann titles were offered. This proved to be an early use of the "shop-within-a-shop" concept.
- *Offering special selections.* Bertelsmann deployed sales representatives to sell books to end users. Cartons of thematically related books — which came to be known as special selections — were developed for this purpose. The sales reps' bonuses were designed to promote sales of cartons over individual books. The result was a significant increase in distribution efficiency.
- *Developing the two-stage club.* Bertelsmann did not invent book clubs. However, it did create a unique variation, the "two-stage book club," by arranging with direct distribution companies and retail bookstores to take responsibility for sales, advertising, and customer care and delivery. Meanwhile, Bertelsmann retained control of selecting the titles, creating the advertising and brand identity, and developing the catalogues. This partnership system enabled Bertelsmann to keep its logistics and other costs lower

than those of its competitors and to pass the savings on to club subscribers.

■ *Centralizing customer care and logistics.* Eventually, as the number of subscribers grew, Bertelsmann's two-stage partnership arrangement proved inefficient. The company responded by setting up a central customer-care and logistics organization, which was slowly and reluctantly accepted by distributors.

By the mid-1950s, the revised organizational structure, which remains largely unchanged today, was fully in place. The number of club members and amount of profit increased at an astounding rate. Soon, however, the limits to domestic growth became apparent and Bertelsmann set out to make its mark on the global market. Its first step was to extend the club system beyond Germany to Austria and Switzerland. Then, in the 1960s, it expanded elsewhere in Western Europe, particularly in the Iberian Peninsula.

Today, Bertelsmann has club systems in more than 16 countries. The foreign share of total turnover exceeded the domestic share by the end of the 1960s, and foreign sales now add up to more than 70% of total sales. By 1995, Bertelsmann boasted 21 million book-club members, with over $4.1 billion in sales.

Challenges for the Club Business

Four distinct trends are revolutionizing the retail book and recording businesses.

Technological Changes

Finally, technological leaps are affecting the book and recording businesses in numerous ways. The alternatives offered by electronic publishing are changing book-production processes.

Marketing via interactive media is revolutionizing the distribution channels in the book industry. Bertelsmann CEO Thomas Middelhoff believes that in the very near term, 50% of the company's turnover will be in the electronic media industry. This prediction is based in reality: established retailers and entrepreneurial newcomers alike are selling books and recordings directly via the Internet, and it is already possible to download music and reading material via the Internet.

Interactive books are one result: as with some computer games, the reader decides how the story continues. Cable-TV channels have also become venues for aggressive sales campaigns that push exclusive offers. Consequently, publishers need to cope with the reality that traditional books and recordings could eventually become superfluous, and only those publishers who embrace new Internet-based operations and products will continue to achieve the success they have enjoyed in the past.

Price and Cost Pressure

There is a growing trend toward budget books. The market share of paperbacks, which often cost only one third the price of retail hardcover books, is increasing. The pricing of high-quality hardcovers has come under pressure from aggressive book dealers and shippers. New competitors are entering the book publishing and music recording businesses to cross-sell products tied to movies and other media. Online bookstores, most notably Amazon.com and Bertelsmann subsidiary barnesandnoble.com, have engaged in their own price war, each trying to undercut the other on the prices of best-selling books, and secondhand bookstores are playing a more important role, offering returned or defective books at low prices.

Dangers also exist on the cost side, particularly given the fluctuating price of paper. Moreover, the ability of publishers to negotiate with authors is deteriorating. "Global authors" — writers whose names alone are enough to secure best-seller status — are emerging. A striking example is John Grisham, who has more than 60 million novels in print worldwide, translated into 29 languages. The changes don't stop there.

Customers' New Buying Criteria

Customers are becoming more difficult to please as other media increasingly demand their attention. Consequently, in many segments, fewer and fewer books are sold each year because the number of potential readers is declining.

New motives for buying are also emerging. Businesses now buy books and recordings in bulk as gifts. This has resulted in specific requirements for both the content and the looks of the books — once the domain of the publisher. Buyers frequently are more interested in a book's design or the originality of its theme than in its actual contents.

Changes in the Competitive Landscape

Pressure on price has fostered concentration within the industry. Smaller providers have left the market or are being bought out. Their acquirers — increasingly, superstores with incredible clout — are hoping to achieve economies of scale to safeguard their market positions.

The same circumstances are motivating publishers to offer specialized product mixes. Some companies believe that by identifying and appealing to specific customer groups with homogeneous needs, they can gain market leadership within a niche. The trend toward specialization exists primarily among the established competitors. Increasing numbers of new entrants are attempting to break into niche markets, which leads to even more price pressure.

―――――――――――――――▲▼▲―――――――――――――――

CONFRONTING THE EROSION OF TRADITIONAL ADVANTAGES

Although Bertelsmann continues to flourish, the entire book industry is under severe competitive pressure. The new trends pose a serious danger to the book club business and could erode its current value to customers. Bertelsmann and other traditional firms need to contend with threats to the following established competitive advantages:

- *Price advantage.* Throughout the book market, pricing structures are under siege. Bertelsmann offers its club members significant price advantages on hardcover books only. However, the club's hardcover editions cost more than paperback versions of the same titles. As long as the club retains the hardback format as its standard, it will have difficulty competing in paperback price sectors.
- *Convenience.* The convenience of club membership is endangered in two ways. First, the mail-order book business, including shopping over the Internet is growing at a tremendous rate. It offers customers just as much convenience as a club, but without the obligation to buy a specific number of titles from a preset list. Second, despite the threat of Internet sales, the retail book business is booming. The bookselling superstores may not be able to offer the convenience of shopping at home, but they are increasingly

providing an entertaining shopping experience. Bookstore super-stores offer an almost unlimited number of titles, set among coffee bars, book groups, and authors' readings, all designed to increase traffic and make customers value their visits to the stores.

■ *Selection*. Mail-order booksellers are just as skilled in selecting titles as clubs are. Moreover, customers are highly knowledge-able about their areas of special interest. Increasingly, niche customers do not need the clubs to act as intermediaries to screen selections.

WORLD-CLASS PERFORMANCE PROGRAM

To defend and enhance its competitive position, Bertelsmann intro-duced a World-Class Performance Program, which is made up of four key components:

1. *World-class standards* presupposes that benchmarking world-class standards will help obtain the overriding growth objectives. For example, improving customer relations requires that indi-vidual consumer groups be targeted with specific products. World-class companies in this regard are typically found in highly competitive industries, such as in clothing manufacturing or insurance. The same challenges exist for mail-order compa-nies and for the Bertelsmann Club, which sends its catalogs to several million members.

2. *Cross-functional concepts* help Bertelsmann reach its world-class goals. The national Bertelsmann Clubs are typically organized by function. This means that responsibilities for customer care, marketing, program development, sales, and logistics are han-dled independently in each club. To achieve world-class status under this structure, all functional areas must change. For exam-ple, the call center must develop detailed, flexible customer data and keep it up to date. The marketing department must continuously perform statistical evaluations and develop group-specific marketing strategies adapted to the most current cus-tomer needs. Program development and the sales department must be equally flexible to execute suitable strategies. Of course, for all this to happen simultaneously, functional department heads must have been convinced of the appropriateness of process transformation.

3. *International know-how transfer* is especially critical to an organization that has operations around the globe, as does Bertelsmann. Cooperation among the national book clubs has greatly enhanced the creativity of new ideas developed at Bertelsmann. Once a new concept has proved effective in one location, it tends to be more readily accepted in other locations. For example, the American and British clubs were the first to offer targeted products under different brand names. Bertelsmann Clubs now uses this concept in other countries, allowing for differences in the specific characteristics of the each national market.

4. *Continuous learning* underscores that no single project can increase the core competence of the book-club business. Rather, the management of core competence must be institutionalized over the long term. A mail-order dealer that uses mass-marketing methods to target its products to specific groups of consumers must continually adjust its assortments. The more intensive the attempt to target specific offerings, the greater the cost of complexity, and the lower the resulting margins. When a mail-order dealer wants to distinguish a product for a specific target group, it often creates a new brand name. Building the new brand's identity may require the creation of a special catalog, with resulting marketing and mailing costs. The ensuing redundancies also drive up the costs of computer processing, customer care, and logistics.

Thus, there are limits to the strategy of targeting specific groups, and these limits — and the resulting costs — can be difficult to determine in advance. Bertelsmann has learned to execute promising marketing concepts more quickly in the national clubs by using what it learns in one country to guide its decisions in the next.

CENTRALIZATION IN A DECENTRALIZED STRUCTURE

Bertelsmann was faced with conflicting demands. The management of core competence must be centralized, yet operations in the book industry require decentralized structures. For example, the global book market is highly fragmented, due, of course, to differences in language. Different markets have different product preferences, and product mixes must be designed accordingly. The national rules of the business vary greatly from country to country, as does the significance of various distribution channels.

To balance its conflicting needs for centralization and decentralization, Bertelsmann created a matrix process organization that operates across the functions of the regional line organizations. The unit responsible for European club business, and thus for the management of core competence, is outside the country-based line structure and reports directly to the chairman of the board. The core competence managers are organized along the business processes identified in the value chain, which adds the advantage of individual specialization.

LOOKING TO THE FUTURE

Bertelsmann began its World-Class Performance Program only 2 years ago, so it is still too early to draw firm conclusions. However, the company has already gained the following valuable insights:

- *Continued growth requires considerable time and patience.* Bertelsmann has been involved in the club business for more than 50 years. Its experience leads to the conclusion that identifying and expanding areas of expertise for future growth requires a thoughtful look at company's history and careful planning.
- *Managing core competencies must be linked to customer needs.* Orienting business strategy to core competence may seem to be a matter of course. However, unless areas of competence are also linked to customer needs, the rapidly transforming market will leave the company behind. Today, changes in market competition make it especially necessary for organizations to continuously refine and revitalize their core competencies.
- *Developing core competence requires strategies such as benchmarking, process orientation, and teaming.* Even when a company has succeeded in developing its core competencies over the long term, as is the case at Bertelsmann, it must be willing to leave the past behind and use modern methods to remain competitive in an ever-changing and demanding marketplace.

ABOUT THE AUTHORS

Jürgen Haritz holds the position of executive vice president human resources of Bertelsmann Book Corporation in Guetersloh, and he is a member of the Board. Dr. Haritz joined Bertelsmann in 1987 and became responsible for the firm's international club division. He was appointed executive vice president in 1993. Dr. Haritz has published several articles and speeches on strategic management compensation policy and also teaches at the University of Portmond.

Andrej Vizjak serves as the executive vice president and chief purchasing officer of Bertelsmann in Munich. His primary area of responsibility include central purchasing, production, and logistics. Prior to joining Bertelsmann, Dr. Vizjak worked at A.T. Kearney from 1990 to 1995, specializing in strategy and organization. He also holds a Ph.D. in strategic management from the University of Munich.

CASE 8

THE PORT OF SINGAPORE

By

Khoo Teng Chye

Tongkangs to Transshipment

THE GROWTH OF THE PORT OF SINGAPORE AUTHORITY

World War II reduced Singapore to ruins, but it could not destroy the vision of the Port of Singapore Authority. In defiance of nay-saying experts and financiers, its leaders were determined to build a modern, world-class port. They had the foresight to look beyond their country's borders and their industry to identify and develop the skills their organization would need to achieve hypergrowth. Then, by blending superior customer service with cutting-edge information technology, they transformed their war-battered port into the world's number one transshipment superhub. The elements at the heart of the organization's strategic vision — attention to customers' needs, modern management practices, continual learning, and an adaptable business culture — have enabled it to enjoy compounded average annual revenue growth of 10.4% since 1964 and lay a firm foundation for global expansion.

PHOENIX FROM THE ASHES

Singapore's skyscrapers tower over some of the busiest shipping lanes and the most efficient container port in the world. The view, however, hasn't always been so impressive. More than 50 years ago, at the end of World War II, Singapore and its harbor stood in near ruins after 3 years of enemy occupation. Having served as the entrepôt port to Southeast Asia since 1819, the port was crippled; its major gateway, Keppel Harbour, suffered massive damage to its machinery, dockyard equipment, and 70% of its warehouses. But the Port of Singapore was committed to building a modern, world-class port out of the wartime ruins and thus began a growth spurt that continues today.

With vision and courage, the leaders fulfilled their mission and transformed the port from a bombed-out shell to a modern, world-class shipping superhub. In October 1997, the Port of Singapore Authority spun off its terminal operations into an independent company: PSA Corporation Limited (PSA). PSA now stands as the largest cargo-transshipment port in the world, with a network of terminals and shipping logistics services around the globe. Its importance transcends Southeast Asia, and beyond.

FARSIGHTED DECISION

As a newly created nation in 1965, Singapore faced many troubles. Having separated from Malaysia amid riots and strife, Singapore was cut off from its natural hinterland and had few natural resources. The young city-state's leaders quickly perceived that Singapore's port was a key infrastructure element on which the new nation would depend.

To succeed, one of its biggest challenges was to catch up with the technology of other worldwide ports. In the 1960s, worldwide shipping practices underwent rapid change. PSA's leaders saw that building a container port, a major high-tech step forward, was the key to the harbor's future. They anticipated correctly the huge wave of containerization that would change the way shipping came to Asia.

Despite the promises of success, the challenges to building a container port proved numerous and daunting.

The first and foremost challenge was to raise the necessary funds. Building and operating a container terminal required a huge investment, and the World Bank was reluctant to provide help. The bank's consultants argued that the region was unprepared for containerization and Singapore's developing economy required only low-tech port facilities.

At home, PSA faced other hurdles. Accustomed to operating in an industry with a global history of poor labor relations and harsh working conditions, the powerful Singapore Port Workers' Union was understandably concerned for its members. The young Singapore government believed that the high unemployment rate called for projects that would create jobs, not replace them with technology.

Against those odds, PSA took a calculated risk to spend millions of dollars to build a container terminal. Through determination, diplomacy, and compelling analysis, PSA won over the opposing parties and opened its first container terminal in Singapore in June 1972.

The risk paid off, and the company experienced legendary growth. It is the first and only container terminal operator in the world to have handled more than 100 million TEUs (20-foot equivalent units). Between 1972 and 1997, PSA enjoyed compounded annual growth of more than 28% in container throughput. Even when confronted with the Asian economic crisis in 1998, PSA marked 7% growth. Dr. Yeo Ning Hong, chairman of PSA Corporation Limited, attributes PSA's strong showing to its emphasis on customer service. "PSA continues to seek out new ways of serving our customers, putting our total resources at the disposal of our customers, customizing procedures and processes to meet all the requirements of individual customers, and helping them maintain their competitive edge in their different market segments," he says. For example, PSA has worked closely with individual customers to help them use the port's resources more effectively, and to lower their operating costs in Singapore.

BENCHMARKING WORLD CLASS

There is, of course, more than one reason for PSA's astounding success. The port executives knew that merely building a modern container terminal was not enough. The organization needed to develop the competencies necessary for an efficient operation — competencies that initially lay entirely outside Singapore. To compensate, PSA sent its young officers to New York and Rotterdam for training in container port management.

PSA recognized that the role of a transshipment hub is to enable shipping economies of scale. Instead of shipping cargo directly to a multitude of destinations, shipping lines can move their cargo to a regional hub. Cargo from multiple shippers can then be broken down and reconsolidated for shipment to the final destination (see Figure 1). PSA was convinced that developing core competencies in superior customer service was the way to turn Singapore into the port of choice on the European and Asian shipping lanes and become the world's

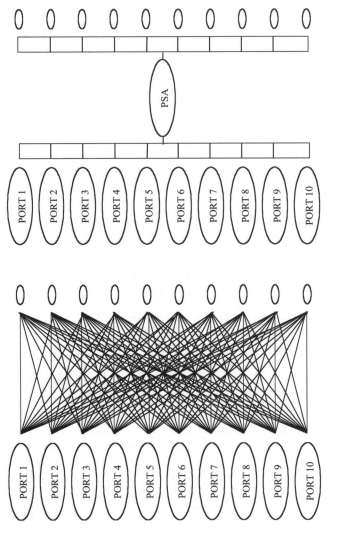

Without transshipment, each port needs a direct service to each other port, thus making a total of 100 (10x10) trips.

Instead of linking directly to every port, each port is transshipped through PSA, dramatically reducing the number of trips to 20 (10+10).

Figure 1   The Superhub Concept.

port of call. Its goal was to make its service and efficiency so out-standing that customers would choose to transship cargo through Singapore rather than ship directly to destination ports.

PSA did this by focusing on the following three broad areas of shipping needs:

- *Reliability.* PSA offers reliability in both scheduling and container handling.
- *Connectivity.* The port offers a wide choice of departures, with frequent sailings and numerous destinations. PSA currently provides connections to 740 ports in 130 countries. On an average day, PSA sends 3 ships to the United States, 4 to Japan, 5 to Europe, and 22 to South Asia and Southeast Asia.
- *Flexibility.* PSA develops value-added, customized solutions tailored to customers' specific needs, such as just-in-time ship-to-ship transfer for containers that have an urgent time-to-market schedule.

To achieve these features, PSA updated all areas of its business technology. For example, no ports were taking advantage of cutting-edge information technology, yet transshipping required increasingly complex logistical operations. To gain insights and increase performance standards, PSA benchmarked global IT leaders, including airlines and banks, then proceeded to develop world-class IT competencies. As a result, PSA now furnishes near-zero-defect logistical operations.

As PSA's service levels and efficiency improved, more and more shipping lines have concentrated on Singapore as a hub. The subsequent critical mass has created more sailings to more destinations, which has further enhanced the hub's attractiveness.

Technological innovation and advances have played a major role in supporting PSA's astounding growth. For example, when increasing Singapore land values resulted in higher costs for dockside storage, PSA met this challenge by developing impressive technological advances to optimize land use. The port now has the ability to stack containers up to nine high, whereas most other ports stack only 2 high.

With some 100,000 containers in the stacking yards at any one time and mother vessels discharging containers to an average of 50 other carriers, moving the boxes between ships is a complex process. To increase efficiency, PSA created advanced equipment and information technology, including an artificial intelligence system that allows one driver to operate three cranes from a remote station. In the early years, PSA sought only to invest in tried and tested technology. Today, from a follower, PSA has become the industry leader in technological competencies.

PSA also recognized the need to outsource low-value-added competencies, such as stevedoring. In each outsourcing case, PSA supports the development of the most efficient process. It sets, measures, and enforces rigorous service standards, working closely with suppliers to improve performance. PSA's record is so successful in these areas that many shipping lines see the port's ability to perform record-breaking turnarounds as an opportunity to make up for time lost elsewhere. For example, the rapid turnaround time in Singapore can enable ships delayed elsewhere to reach their time window at the Suez Canal's one-way traffic system.

PSA's world-class customer service proves to be a winner for its customers and for itself. It achieved an annually compounded average revenue growth of 10.4% since 1964 and an average return on fixed assets of 13% since 1989. (In most infrastructure investments, 9% is considered a solid return.)

Many analysts see PSA's customer service and business excellence as creations of its superior technology and functional skills. PSA is certainly the world leader in port operations equipment technology and integrating complex operations using information technology. However, reducing PSA to its technical competencies is too simplistic. At the heart of PSA's astounding growth and leadership position lie the following crucial elements of the firm's strategic vision:

- *Attention to customers' needs.* PSA strives to meet the needs of its customers and to enhance its customers' competitiveness and profitability.
- *Best-practice management.* PSA benchmarks global and cross-industry best practices, and involves staff from all levels and fields to contribute to improved productivity.
- *Continuous learning.* PSA institutionalizes the improvement of its core processes through its operations planning department, human resource development department, organizational development, department, and the PSA Institute, a corporate university.
- *An adaptable business culture.* Many organizations find it difficult to create a business culture that pursues continuous improvement,

and find it even more difficult to translate that culture to new ventures and related businesses. PSA has established methods of extending its world-class competencies to all its operations. PSA's challenge is to get the entire organization to move with the mindset of anticipating, welcoming, and embracing change.

STAYING AHEAD

It was no small task for PSA to become the world's largest transshipment port. However, the organization faces an even more challenging goal: to maintain its superior position while expanding into other areas. It plans to stay ahead by focusing on three areas: continuous corporate innovation, top-level recruiting, and enhanced organizational development.

One way PSA spurs innovation is through its operations planning department. Founded in 1993 and comprising PSA officers with the requisite skills and brainpower, the department conducts applied research on new technologies.

One of the department's responsibilities is to scout other industries, such as high-tech manufacturing, for competencies and technologies that can help the port grow. The department applies ideas from those industries to specific segments of the container terminal process, for example, using driverless IT-controlled vehicles that follow guide tracks in the pavement to move containers. Because PSA recognizes the growing complexity of its business, it systematically employs its management development program to recruit new officers with a broad range of capabilities. PSA posts its recruits throughout the organization to give them extensive experience in both operational and support functions.

PSA also acknowledges the importance of organizational development by emphasizing its quality circle and staff suggestion programs. PSA aims to create a culture that allows employees from every level to contribute to the enhancement and improvement of work practices.

TWO PATHS TO CONTINUED GROWTH

In the early 1990s, when PSA's senior executives recognized that growth based on trade through the Singapore superhub would reach a plateau, they developed the next step in PSA's business strategy. They decided to focus on two key competencies, port management and shipping logistics, as springboards for global expansion.

They identified other ports along the arterial European–Asian trade route that PSA could invest in and manage, including Aden in Yemen, Genoa in Italy, and Dalian in China. By managing those ports, the company is creating a network advantage that simultaneously enhances the role of its own superhub and builds a global PSA brand.

During this process, PSA has been careful to avoid the pitfalls inherent in moving operations to other cultures and locations. The organization is working hard to globalize its management team and to open the PSA Institute, its training school, to managers from all of its ports. PSA will progressively cross-deploy staff among its operations. For example, it might post Italian officers at the Dalian Container Terminal in China and Chinese officers at the Voltri Terminal Europa.

Because sovereign states often see ports as national assets rather than businesses, the port realizes that nationalism could become a significant obstacle to expansion. To alleviate this, PSA uses its Chinese, Italian, and English cultural and language skills to help overcome resistance to its investments. PSA also contains local political risk by maintaining good labor relations. For example, when PSA built Singapore's container terminal, it avoided layoffs by retraining and redeploying its workers. Those workers are now among the most productive port labor forces in the world and, as a result, enjoy the benefits of superior wages and greater job security. PSA's history of progressive labor practices sends a powerful message to the host governments and potentially hostile unions in possible investment locations.

PSA's second strategy for growth takes advantage of its strength in logistics. Because Asian supply chains often restrict business growth, PSA can find many opportunities to apply its logistical skills. For example, in partnering with Horst Mosolf, the German specialist in automotive logistics, PSA is using its skills in warehouse management to bring predelivery inspection and installation to Singapore.

WHAT'S NEXT?

For the past 50 years, PSA has consistently demonstrated how to grow, sustain, and renew corporate excellence. The organization focuses its resources, skills, technologies, and strategies on competitive advantages that will generate business success through customer satisfaction. In the words of PSA's chairman, Dr. Yeo Ning Hong, "Our competencies are worthwhile only if they are of value to our customers."

Today, PSA faces the short-term consequences of the Asian economic crisis and its impact on container trade. However, the company realizes that this is neither the first turbulence in its history nor will it be the last. Over the past three and a half decades, the port has achieved tremendous growth in container volume, revenue, productivity, and return on investment. It is now leveraging its competencies to pursue even more growth in a future that lies beyond Singapore and beyond port management.

ABOUT THE AUTHOR

Khoo Teng Chye is the Group President of the PSA Corporation Limited. He served in the Urban Redevelopment Authority from 1976 to 1996 and became its chief executive officer/chief planner in 1992. Previously, he was with the Singapore Administrative Service between 1995 and 1998. For his public service, Mr. Khoo was awarded the country's Silver Public Administration Medal in 1987 and the Gold Public Administration Medal in 1996.

Conclusion

IGNITING THE GROWTH ENGINES

Brian Harrison

Growth creates value. Findings in a broad-based global study by A.T. Kearney confirm it. Companies with conscious commitments to sustained growth have increased their shareholder value by 26% per year, compared to 16% for companies that focus primarily on profit.

This finding is all the more striking because, as the examples described in this book illustrate, value-building growth is possible in any industry, in any region, and at any phase of the business cycle. These companies have continually redefined their markets and reinvented themselves.

PUSHING THE ENVELOPE

The A.T. Kearney study found that, like most of our case study companies, value growers emphasize innovation, expansion, and risk taking. They push the envelope in all three areas, whether it is applied to internally generated growth or to external growth through mergers and acquisitions. For example, their appetite and eye for innovation lead them to invest four times (on average) as much in "white-space" opportunities as other companies.

Value growers also pursue geographic expansion far more aggressively than their competitors. Their international sales account for one third of their overall growth, twice the rate of other companies. They focus on securing and stretching their core competencies. They avoid blind, wide-scale diversification and draw the bulk of their revenues and profits by building on their cores. They do not divert funds from a successful business to bolster performance gains in other businesses.

SHARED DRIVERS BEHIND VALUE-BUILDING GROWTH

Despite their different industries and strategies, the value growers identified in the A.T. Kearney study share a common set of drivers, which they use to keep their growth engines accelerating. Much like primates, a family whose DNA is over 90% identical, value growers share a common heritage, an advanced "corporate DNA" that increases their chances of survival and success. Indeed, the majority of value growers attribute almost 90% of their success to the use of internal drivers to actively steer and manage growth. These internal drivers found in our study parallel closely those cited by our case study authors and include the following:

- *Growth vision.* As this book has amply illustrated, a vision for growth is said to be the single most important internal driver. Of the companies surveyed, 83% of value growers have a growth vision that is well defined, ambitious, and well communicated. More than half said this vision was the turning point that drove them toward new-found growth. Almost three quarters of executives from value-building growth companies could articulate a clear and focused strategy, while only 27% of the others could do so. Value growers have a firm understanding of their core business and frequently make acquisitions to grow that core, and *only* that core. They rarely succumb to the temptation to take on a new business sector. Similarly, they know when to leave a market that is no longer strategic, as Braun did in the case of the audio products business.
- *Customer focus.* As for our case study companies, the customer comes first for all value growers. Based on their customer and market intelligence, value growers constantly seek ways to enhance their interactions with their existing customers and capture new ones. From the company's basic value proposition and its use of creative pricing to increasing its online presence, a value grower makes the most of its opportunities to interact with customers.

- *Operational excellence.* A company cannot sustain growth if its internal organization, information technology, and processes do not grow and improve as well. Our study found that value growers set milestones that let them know when an organizational overhaul is due. They implement processes that encourage and exploit cross-functional communication and knowledge sharing. Parallel to investing in their own R&D, they invest heavily and wisely in IT because it positions them for future growth. Finally, these companies follow the motto "What gets measured gets done."
- *Culture.* For growth to endure over the long term, there needs to be an open and progressive *culture.* The highest growth rates belong to companies whose internal cultures promote customer service and the ability to meet customers' needs. Empowerment, open communication, and a competitive spirit characterize a value-building culture. Motorola's emphasis on creating a culture that gives voice to minority, and even dissenting, viewpoints has contributed significantly to its ability to create and innovate.
- *Resource allocation.* All CEOs understand the importance of securing key resources to establish their competency in a particular field. The key is in how they allocate their resources. Take, for example, the different ways high-growth companies handle their research and development costs during business downturns. When earnings are squeezed, companies that focus on the bottom line almost always force down their budgets, while value growers extend their resources and maintain the same investments in R&D even during hard times, as Bristol-Myers Squibb did.

The eight companies profiled here have mastered the skills they need to survive and thrive in changing times. Companies will always face new and difficult challenges that will require hard work, innovation, and creativity to overcome. A growth vision to motivate and guide a company into the future is key. To turn the vision into reality, a company must be able to learn new skills, new techniques, new "everything" on an ongoing basis. The customer is the ultimate judge and juror of a company's success and, as such, must be treated as a top priority.

Finally, companies must reach for excellence. Above all else, these eight companies have demonstrated that whatever trials they face, their dedication to excellence has served — and will continue to serve — as a competitive advantage that will guide their continued growth and success.